Good Practice in Rational Emotive Behaviour Therapy

Good Practice in Rational Emotive Behaviour Therapy does exactly what it promises. It helps the Rational Emotive Behaviour Therapy (REBT) therapist to pinpoint areas of good practice enabling them to make progress towards becoming competent practitioners.

Instead of focusing on what not to do in practice, this revised second edition instead emphasises what to do. Covering 101 areas of good practice, this thoroughly updated second edition places emphasis on developing and maintaining the therapeutic alliance, how to outline REBT for potential clients so that they can make an informed decision about whether to engage with the service and how to prepare clients to carry out their tasks in the therapy. A new focus is also placed on online therapy.

This highly accessible and practical book is an indispensable guide for anyone embarking on a career in the REBT field.

Windy Dryden is in clinical and consultative practice and is an international authority on Single-Session Therapy and Rational Emotive Behaviour Therapy. He has worked in psychotherapy for more than 45 years and is the author or editor of over 275 books.

Good Practice in Rational Emotive Behaviour Therapy

Second Edition

Windy Dryden

Routledge
Taylor & Francis Group
LONDON AND NEW YORK

Second edition published 2025
by Routledge
4 Park Square, Milton Park, Abingdon, Oxon, OX14 4RN

and by Routledge
605 Third Avenue, New York, NY 10158

Routledge is an imprint of the Taylor & Francis Group, an informa business

First edition published by Routledge 2012 under the title *Learning from Mistakes in Rational Emotive Behaviour Therapy*

British Library Cataloguing-in-Publication Data
A catalogue record for this book is available from the British Library

Library of Congress Cataloging-in-Publication Data
Title: Good practice in rational emotive behaviour therapy / Windy Dryden.
Other titles: Learning from mistakes in rational emotive behaviour therapy
Description: Second edition. | Abingdon, Oxon ; New York, NY : Routledge, 2025. |
Preceded by Learning from mistakes in rational emotive behaviour therapy /
Windy Dryden and Michael Neenan. 2012. |
Includes bibliographical references and index. |
Identifiers: LCCN 2024021805 (print) | LCCN 2024021806 (ebook) |
ISBN 9781032729893 (hardback) | ISBN 9781032729862 (paperback) |
ISBN 9781003423348 (ebook)
Subjects: MESH: Psychotherapy, Rational-Emotive–methods
Classification: LCC RC489.R3 (print) | LCC RC489.R3 (ebook) |
NLM WM 420.5.P8 | DDC 616.89/14–dc23/eng/20240624
LC record available at https://lccn.loc.gov/2024021805
LC ebook record available at https://lccn.loc.gov/2024021806

ISBN: 9781032729893 (hbk)
ISBN: 9781032729862 (pbk)
ISBN: 9781003423348 (ebk)

DOI: 10.4324/9781003423348

Typeset in Times New Roman
by Newgen Publishing UK

Contents

Preface

In the previous edition of the book, with the different title, *Learning from Mistakes in Rational Emotive Behaviour Therapy*, my co-author Michael Neenan and I wanted to address a number of errors that therapists and trainees make in the practice of Rational Emotive Behaviour Therapy (REBT) and show how these can be avoided. In the second edition of this book (which I have written by myself), I wanted to change the focus and tone of the work. Rather than focus on mistakes and how they can be avoided, I wanted to concentrate on outlining what is good practice in REBT and how this can be implemented with clients.

After providing an introduction to REBT, I have divided the book into eight parts: general good practice, good practice in assessing clients' problems, good practice in goal-setting, good practice in encouraging clients to examine their attitudes, good practice in negotiating and reviewing homework tasks, good practice in dealing with clients' doubts, reservations and objections to REBT, good practice in the working-through phase of REBT and good practice in self-maintenance. The dialogue excerpts in the book are not verbatim accounts of therapy or supervision but illustrative examples of the points being made.

It is my hope that training and trained REBT therapists will be able to use the points made in this book to enhance their own good practice of REBT.

Windy Dryden
London and Eastbourne
January 2024

Introduction to Rational Emotive Behaviour Therapy

In this brief introduction to REBT, I will outline some of its major theoretical and practical features. This will help people unfamiliar with REBT to get the most from this book.

REBT's Distinctive *Situational ABC* Framework

While an *ABC* framework for understanding psychological problems can be found in different approaches to Cognitive Behaviour Therapy (CBT), REBT (one of the earliest approaches within the CBT tradition) uses a distinctive *Situational ABC* framework. In this framework, the person is deemed to disturb themself at *C* about an aspect of the *situation* that they are in (known as the adversity at *A*) primarily because they hold a set of rigid and extreme basic attitudes at *B* (Dryden 2021a). For example:

Situation	My boss left a note on my desk asking me to see him as soon as possible
A (Adversity)	My boss is going to criticise me for something that I have done
B (Basic Attitude)	*(rigid basic attitude)* = My boss must not criticise me *(extreme basic attitude)* = If my boss criticises me that would be terrible
C (Consequence)	*(emotional)* = Anxious *(behavioural)* = Wanting to run away = Takes a sedative before going to see boss *(cognitive)* = My boss will look for ways to fire me = I will find it hard to get another job because my boss will not give me a good reference

DOI: 10.4324/9781003423348-1

While the above outlines REBT's *Situational ABC* framework explaining psychological disturbance, the following outlines REBT's *Situational ABC* framework explaining a psychologically healthy response to the same adversity at *A*. Here, the person is deemed to respond healthily at *C* about the same adversity at *A* largely because they hold a set of flexible and non-extreme basic attitudes at *B* (Dryden 2021a).

Situation	My boss left a note on my desk asking me to see him as soon as possible
A (*Adversity*)	My boss is going to criticise me for something that I have done
B (*Basic Attitude*)	(*flexible basic attitude*) = I do not want my boss to criticise me, but that does not mean that he must not do so (*non-extreme basic attitude*) = If my boss criticises me that would be bad, but not terrible
C (*Consequence*)	(*emotional*) = Concerned (*behavioural*) = Wanting to face up to what my boss has to say without taking any medication (*cognitive*) = If my boss is unhappy with something I have done, he will tell me, but he probably will not look for ways to fire me

This framework has several distinctive features:

1. *A* is often inferential in nature. Inferences are deemed to go beyond the data at hand and may be accurate or inaccurate. In the absence of finding out the 'truth' about what happened, the person may be encouraged to make the 'best bet' given the available data. As will be shown later, in order to identify rigid and extreme attitudes at *B*, practitioners of REBT first encourage their clients to assume temporarily that *A* is true and will work with distorted inferences at *A* after the clients have made progress at changing rigid and extreme attitudes at *B* to their flexible and non-extreme attitude alternatives.

2. As shown above, basic attitudes at *B* are the central determining factor of functional and dysfunctional responses at *C* about adversities at *A*.
3. *C* can be emotive, behavioural and cognitive.
4. *ABCs* are best understood within a situational context.

Emphasis on Attitudes

Perhaps the central tenet of REBT theory is that rigid attitudes are at the very core of psychological disturbance. Ellis (1994) argued that while what he called irrational beliefs (or what I call 'attitudes') can be rigid or extreme, of the two, it is rigid attitudes that are at the very core of disturbance. Rigid attitudes are often based on preferences but are then transformed into absolutes. Thus, if I hold that it is important to me that you like me, then this is my preference. When I make this preference rigid, I transform it into a demand, thus: 'I want you to like me, and therefore you must do so'. It is important to note that rigid attitudes are often expressed without the preference being made explicit, thus: 'You must like me'.

REBT theory posits that rigid attitudes are at the very core of disturbance (Ellis 1994). As such, other dysfunctional attitudes and distorted cognitions are derived from this rigid core. Extreme attitudinal derivatives are the closest derivatives to this core. REBT theory argues that there are three extreme attitudinal derivatives from rigid attitudes. In the material that follows, I will list and define each extreme attitude and show that it is derived from the person's rigid attitude. These extreme attitudes are known as:

1. *Awfulising attitudes*. Here, the client believes at the time of disturbance that something is so bad that it could not get any worse. For example: 'You must like me, and it would be absolutely awful if you do not'.
2. *Attitudes of unbearability*. Here, the client holds that they cannot bear the adversity that they are facing or about to face. For example: 'You must like me, and I could not bear it if you do not'.
3. *Devaluation attitudes*. Here the client gives themself, others or life a global negative evaluation which, at the time, they think defines them, others or life. For example, 'You must like me, and if you do not, I'm not worthy'.

The corollary of the point that rigid attitudes are at the very core of psychological disturbance is that flexible attitudes are at the very core of psychological health. Ellis (1994) argued that while what he called rational attitudes can be flexible or non-extreme, of the two, it is flexible attitudes that are at the very core of psychological health. Flexible attitudes, like rigid attitudes, are often based on preferences, but they are flexible because the person is explicit that they are not rigid. Thus, if I hold that it is important to me that you like me, then this is again my preference. When I keep this preference flexible, I negate the demand, thus: 'I want you to like me, but you do not have to do so'.

REBT theorists also argue that non-extreme attitudes and realistic cognitions are derived from flexible attitudes (Ellis 1994). Non-extreme attitudinal derivatives are the closest derivatives to this core. REBT theorists argue that there are three non-extreme attitudinal derivatives from flexible attitudes. In the material that follows, I will list and define each non-extreme attitude and show that it is derived from the person's flexible attitude. These non-extreme attitudes are known as:

1. *Non-awfulising attitudes*. Here the client holds at the time that something is bad, but not the end of the world. For example: 'I want you to like me, but you do not have to do so. It is bad that you do not, but not awful'.
2. *Attitudes of bearability*. Here the client holds that it is difficult bearing the adversity that they are facing or about to face, but that they can bear it and that it is worth it for them to do so. Also, they assert that they are willing to tolerate the adversity and commit themself to so doing. For example: 'I want you to like me, but you do not have to do so. It would be difficult for me to tolerate you not liking me, but I can tolerate it, and it is worth doing so. I am willing to bear you not liking me and will commit myself to do so by facing you'.
3. *Unconditional acceptance attitudes*. Here the client acknowledges that they, others or life are far too complex to merit a global negative evaluation and that such an evaluation does not define them, others or life. For example, 'I want you to like me, but you do not have to do so. I am the same fallible person whether you like me or not'.

REBT's Position on Negative Emotions

REBT theorists distinguish between unhealthy (dysfunctional) negative emotions and healthy (functional) negative emotions. They argue that unhealthy negative emotions and healthy negative emotions are qualitatively different from one another as unhealthy negative emotions stem from rigid and extreme attitudes toward adversity, and healthy negative emotions stem from flexible and non-extreme attitudes towards the same adversity (see Dryden 2022a). As such, these distinguishable emotions exist on two separate continua rather than on one single continuum.

For example, anxiety about a threat is underpinned by a rigid and extreme attitude towards the adversity, and its healthy alternative about that same threat is concern, which is underpinned by a flexible and non-extreme attitude. The goal in REBT is not to reduce the intensity of anxiety; rather, it is to help the person to feel concerned rather than anxious about a threat.

How Clients Create Highly Distorted Inferences: An REBT Perspective

When clients discuss their problems with their REBT therapists, it sometimes occurs that they report highly distorted inferences. Given the available evidence, it is usually readily apparent to the therapist that such inferences are negatively biased and highly skewed to the negative. However, these inferences seem very real to clients. Examples of such inferences are: 'I am going to have a heart attack'; 'Nobody will ever talk to me again'; and 'I will always fail and will end up a bag lady'.

REBT theory argues that such inferences are cognitive consequences (at *C*) of rigid and extreme attitudes (e.g. Dryden et al. 1989). Such inferences are highly distorted because prior related and usually less distorted inferences at *A* have been processed by the person using their rigid and extreme attitudes at *B*. However, the client is usually only aware of the highly distorted inference at *C* as it is very compelling and is usually unaware of both their inference at *A* and their rigid and/or extreme attitude at *B*. Here are three examples of this process. Note how the rigid and the extreme processing of *A* leads to the highly distorted inference at *C*. Thus:

A = I am feeling out of control
B = I must gain control immediately
C (cognitive) = If I do not, I will have a heart attack

A = My friends are not talking to me
B = My friends must talk to me, and it is terrible that they are not
C (cognitive) = Nobody will ever talk to me again

A = I may fail a crucial forthcoming exam
B = I must pass this exam, and it will be the end of the world if I do not
C (cognitive) = If I fail, I will always fail and will end up a bag lady

REBT's Position on Human Worth

REBT theory has a unique position on human worth. Actually, it has two positions on this subject, a preferred position and a back-up position. It holds that unchangeable aspects of humans are our:

1. Humanness (we are human till we die).
2. Complexity (we are too complex to justify a single defining global rating).
3. Uniqueness (there will never be another you).
4. Fallibility (we have an incurable error-making tendency).
5. Changeability (we are constantly in flux).

REBT's preferred position on human worth is that we are neither worthwhile or worthless; rather we just are and we can either choose to accept ourselves as human and as having the above unchangeable aspects or choose not to do so. When we do make this affirmative choice, we can be said to be operationalising a philosophy of unconditional self-acceptance, which encapsulates REBT's preferred position on human worth.

When clients do not resonate with this position and prefer to regard themselves as having worth, then the best way of doing this without making themselves vulnerable to ego disturbance (see below) is to opt for unconditional self-worth. This back-up position states that I am worthwhile because I am human, complex, unique, fallible and changeable. I could, of course, state that I am worthless because I have these aspects, and this is equally valid for I can neither prove that I am worthwhile nor worthless. However, if I want to live healthily and happily, then the unconditional self-worth position will facilitate this far more than the unconditional worthlessness position.

According to REBT, the real culprit (apart from unconditional worthlessness) when it comes to ego disturbance is conditional self-worth. Thus, when a client says 'I am worthwhile when I am loved, successful, popular and wealthy' for example, then they disturb themself when they lose any of these factors, and they are vulnerable to disturbance when they have these factors because they can always lose them.

REBT Differentiates between Ego and Discomfort Disturbance and Health

REBT theorists argue that we have two major domains in which we function as humans: ego and non-ego (here referred to as discomfort). It, therefore, differentiates between ego disturbance and discomfort disturbance, on the one hand, and ego health and discomfort health, on the other.

Ego disturbance in the face of adversity is marked by a rigid attitude and a self-devaluation attitude that is derived from it. For example, a client says, 'I must pass my exam, and I am a failure if I do not'. By contrast, ego health in the face of the same adversity is marked by a flexible attitude and an unconditional self-acceptance attitude that is derived from it. For example, the same client says: 'I would like to pass my exam, but I do not have to do so. If I do not, I am not a failure. I am an unrateable human being who has failed in this respect'.

Discomfort disturbance in the face of adversity is marked by a rigid attitude and an attitude of unbearability that is derived from it. For example, a client says: 'I must have the benefits that I will get if I pass my exam, and I could not bear to be deprived of these benefits should I fail'. By contrast, discomfort health in the face of the same adversity is marked by a flexible attitude and an attitude of bearability that is derived from it. For example, the same client says: 'I would like to have the benefits that I will get if I pass my exam, but I do not need these benefits. If I fail the exam and am thus deprived of these benefits, then it would be a struggle for me to bear this deprivation. However, I could bear it, it is worth it to me to do so, I am willing to do so, and I commit myself to so doing by…'.

There are two other important points worth noting about ego and discomfort disturbance. First, a rigid attitude on its own does not make clear the type of disturbance a person is experiencing. The extreme attitudinal derivative helps to make this clear. Thus, if my rigid attitude is: 'I must retain my autonomy', this attitude, on its own, does not indicate ego or discomfort disturbance. However, if my major extreme attitudinal derivative is: '…and I am a pathetic person if I lose my autonomy', then I am experiencing ego disturbance, whereas if it is: '…and I cannot bear the resultant conditions if I lose of my autonomy', then I am experiencing discomfort disturbance.

The second important point is that ego disturbance and discomfort disturbance frequently interact. Thus, I may begin by experiencing ego disturbance and create a disturbed negative emotion such as shame, and then I may focus on the pain of this emotion and tell myself that I cannot bear this emotional pain (discomfort disturbance).

REBT's Focus on Meta-Disturbance

REBT theorists recognise that once a person disturbs themself, it often happens that they then disturb themself about this original disturbance. This is known as *meta-disturbance* (literally disturbance about disturbance), and I gave an example of this at the end of the previous section. So, REBT has a decided focus on meta-disturbance. It also distinguishes between different types of meta-disturbance. Thus, it argues that a person can disturb themself about:

- Disturbed emotions at *C*. A person may disturb themself either because of the pain of the emotional experience (e.g. I cannot stand the pain of feeling depressed) or because of the meaning the disturbed emotion has for the person (e.g. feeling depressed is a weakness and proves that I am a weak person).

- Dysfunctional behaviour or action tendencies at *C*. Here the person focuses on what they did, or what they felt like doing but did not do, and disturbs themself about one or the other, primarily because of the meaning the behaviour or action tendency has for the person (e.g. I felt like punching her lights out which is really nasty and proves that I am a nasty person).
- Distorted cognitions at *C*. Here, a person may focus on a distorted cognition, which becomes their new *A* and disturbs themself about the meaning that such a thought has for them. Thus, suppose the person disturbs themself about finding a young person attractive and thinks that they may abuse the person (their distorted cognitive consequence at *C*). They may then disturb themself about this thought because they infer that it is shameful and that they are a disgusting person for having it.

REBT's Position on the Origin and Maintenance of Psychological Problems

We have seen that one of the key theoretical principles of REBT is that summarised in the maxim that: 'People are not disturbed by events but by the rigid and extreme attitudes that they hold towards these events'. This means that while adversities contribute to the development of psychological disturbance, mainly when these events are highly aversive, disturbance occurs when people bring their tendencies to hold rigid and extreme attitudes towards these events.

Most approaches to CBT are based on social learning principles, whereby it is held that people learn to disturb themselves. REBT theorists also argue that human disturbance is partly learned, but it is unique among the CBT approaches in claiming that the biological basis of human irrationality and related disturbance is often more influential than its social learning basis. Thus, in a seminal paper, Ellis (1976) put forward several arguments in favour of the 'biological hypothesis' as it is known in REBT circles. Here are a few of Ellis's arguments:

1. People easily transform their strong preferences into rigid demands and have a difficult time giving up these demands and remain with their strong, flexible preferences.

2. People are rarely taught to procrastinate and live self-undisciplined lives, but millions do so.
3. People easily fall back into self-defeating patterns after they have made progress in dealing constructively with these patterns.
4. People can easily give people sound advice in dealing with their problems, but find it difficult to apply this advice consistently to themselves when they experience the same problems.

REBT theorists do not, therefore, have an elaborate view on the origins of disturbance. Having said this, they do acknowledge that it is easy for humans when they are young to disturb themselves about highly aversive events. However, they argue that even under these conditions, people react differently to the same event, and thus, we need to understand what a person brings to and takes from an adversity. People learn their standards and goals from their culture, but disturbance occurs when they bring their rigid and extreme attitudes to circumstances where their standards are not met, and the pursuit of their goals is blocked.

By contrast, REBT theorists have a more elaborate view of how psychological disturbance is maintained. They argue that people perpetuate their disturbance for several reasons, including the following:

- They lack the insight that their psychological disturbance is underpinned by their rigid and extreme attitudes and think instead that events cause it.
- They think that once they understand that their problems are underpinned by rigid and extreme attitudes, this understanding alone will lead to change.
- They do not work persistently to change their rigid and extreme attitudes and to integrate the flexible and non-extreme alternatives to these attitudes into their attitudinal system.
- They continue to act in ways that are consistent with their rigid and extreme attitudes.
- They disturb themselves about their original disturbances.
- They lack or are deficient in critical social skills, communication skills, problem-solving skills and other life skills.
- They think that their disturbance has pay-offs that outweigh the advantages of the healthy alternatives to their disturbed feelings and/or behaviour.

- They live in environments which support the rigid and extreme attitudes that underpin their problems.

As will be seen in the next section REBT's view on the perpetuation of psychological disturbance informs its position on psychological change.

Choice-Based Constructivism and Good Mental Health

REBT theorists favour what might be called choice-based constructivism in that it argues that humans have choices when they hold preferences (e.g. 'I want you to like me'). Thus, they can construct a rigid attitude from this preference ('I want you to like me…and, therefore, you must do so') or a flexible attitude from the same preference (e.g. 'I want you to like me…but you do not have to do so'). Although a person may have a biologically based tendency to construct a rigid attitude when their preference is strong, they do not have to do this and can choose to construct a flexible attitude instead. The extent to which the person does this in a meaningful way depends on the extent to which they are prepared to 'go against the grain' and think and act according to the less powerful flexible attitude preference and refrain from thinking and acting according to their more powerful rigid attitude.

REBT theorists have a clear position on what constitutes good mental health with flexibility and non-extremeness at its heart. Here is a partial list of such criteria which is self-explanatory: personal responsibility; flexibility and anti-extremism; scientific thinking and non-utopian in outlook; enlightened self-interest; social interest; self-direction; high tolerance of uncertainty; strong commitment to meaningful pursuits; calculated risk-taking and long-range hedonism.

REBT's View of Psychological Change

REBT has a realistic view of psychological change and encourages clients to accept that change is hard work, and consequently, it urges therapists to be forceful, energetic and persistent as long as doing so does not threaten the therapeutic alliance (Dryden and Neenan 2004).

It also encourages clients to understand and implement the REBT change process by:

- Realising that they largely create their own psychological problems and that while situations contribute to these problems, they are in general of lesser importance in the change process.
- Fully recognising that they can address and overcome these problems.
- Setting goals.
- Understanding that their problems stem largely from rigid and extreme attitudes and that adopting alternative flexible and non-extreme attitudes will help them to achieve their goals.
- Detecting their rigid and extreme attitudes and discriminating between them and their flexible and non-extreme attitudes.
- Examining their rigid and extreme attitudes and their flexible and non-extreme attitudes until they see clearly that the former are false, illogical and unconstructive while the latter are true, sensible and constructive.
- Working toward the internalisation of their new flexible and non-extreme attitudes by using a variety of cognitive (including imaginal), emotive and behavioural change methods. In particular, clients are advised to act in ways that are consistent with the flexible and non-extreme attitudes that they wish to develop and to refrain from acting in ways that are consistent with their old rigid and extreme attitudes.
- Identifying and dealing with obstacles to change.
- Implementing relapse-prevention procedures.
- Generalising change to other relevant situations.
- Accepting themselves for backsliding and continuing to use REBT change techniques.
- Extending this process of examining attitudes and using multi-modal methods of change into other areas of their lives and committing to doing so for as long as necessary.

REBT's Position on the Importance of the Therapeutic Relationship

The therapeutic relationship in REBT is deemed to be important, but not curative and draws fully on working alliance theory (Bordin 1979) as a way of understanding the importance of bonds, views, goals and tasks in REBT (Dryden 2024). In brief, effectiveness in REBT is enhanced when the therapist and the client:

- Have a well-*bond*ed relationship in which the client experiences the therapist as understanding both their feelings and the attitudes that underpin these feelings, as accepting them as a fallible human being and as genuine in the therapeutic encounter. In this respect, Ellis (in Dryden 1997) cautioned REBT therapists against being overly warm with clients so as not to reinforce the latter's needs for love and approval. In general, REBT therapists consider that client experience of these therapist-offered 'core conditions' (Rogers 1957) are deemed to be important, but neither necessary nor sufficient for enduring client change (Ellis 1959).
- Share common *views* on such matters as problem assessment, 'case' formulation, treatment and practical issues concerning therapy.
- Share an agreed vision concerning client treatment *goals*.
- Understand one another's *tasks* concerning what needs to be done for client goals to be met and can commit to carrying out their respective tasks.

While REBT therapists adopt an active-directive stance in therapy, particularly at its outset, they are not prescriptive about how to implement that stance in terms of therapeutic style. Thus, it is possible for REBT therapists to be informal or formal, humorous or serious, self-disclosing or non-self-disclosing, Socratic or didactic and using metaphors, parables and stories or refraining from their use. Skilful REBT therapists vary their therapeutic style according to the client that they are working with and the stage of therapy that they have reached. Also, while REBT therapists are mindful of the many ways in which their clients differ, they argue that each person is a unique individual and it would be wrong to make assumptions about a person because of their age, race, gender and cultural background, for example. Instead, REBT therapists seek to modify the therapeutic relationship based on the person's unique preferences. A question I routinely ask clients is: 'For me to be most helpful is there anything you feel that is important for me to know about your culture, ethnicity, religion, language, sexual orientation, gender identity/expression, mental or physical health, or another factor?'

REBT's Position on Case Formulation

REBT therapists take a flexible approach to case formulation using this to guide interventions, particularly in complex cases. However, they argue that one can do good therapy without making such a formulation and hold that frequently this formulation can be developed during therapy rather than fully at its outset. However, when a 'case' is deemed to be complicated, or a client is not making expected progress, then doing a more formal extensive case formulation may be indicated (see Dryden 1998, for a full discussion on the REBT approach to case formulation which is outside the scope of this introduction).

REBT's Psychoeducational Emphasis

REBT has a decided psychoeducational emphasis, and its practitioners argue that its theory of disturbance and change, as well as its core concepts, can actively be taught to and learned and implemented by clients. This principle is underpinned by the idea that REBT therapists are very explicit about the REBT model and actively teach it to clients at an early stage so that they can give their informed consent before proceeding with this form of therapy.

While REBT can be practised in many ways, its skills of assessing and addressing problems can be directly taught to clients so that they can learn to be their own therapists almost from the outset. Indeed, some of the materials that have been devised to help clients to learn REBT self-help skills can also be used by people who wish to help themselves without formal therapy (e.g. Dryden 2022b). In addition there are a number of REBT self-help books based on particular themes that also serve the same purpose (e.g. Dryden 1999).

Skilled REBT therapists will work explicitly with clients so that together they can choose whether and when to take a skills-teaching and learning approach to REBT.

REBT's Preferred Treatment Order

REBT recommends a preferred order of treatment and argues that client problems should ideally be dealt with in the following order: (a) disturbance, (b) dissatisfaction, and (c) development. Disturbance is deemed to be present when the client is facing an adversity and holds a set of rigid and extreme attitudes towards that adversity. The resultant dysfunctional ways of responding (emotionally, behaviourally and cognitively) means that the client is ill-equipped to deal with the adversity while they are in a disturbed frame of mind. When they deal successfully with their disturbance, they are then ready to deal with the dissatisfaction of facing the adversity since at this point the client holds a set of flexible and non-extreme attitudes towards the adversity which has now become a focus for dissatisfaction rather than disturbance. Development issues, as the name implies, concern the client exploring ways of developing themself so that they can get the most out of their potential. They will not be able to do this as effectively as they could until they have dealt with the dissatisfaction of having an adversity in their life. Thus, their REBT therapist would encourage them to take steps to change the adversity if it can be changed or adjust constructively to the adversity if it can't be changed – while holding flexible and non-extreme attitudes, rather than rigid and extreme attitudes – before focusing their attention on development issues, if the client is seeking help in this area. Such work might be better described as REB coaching rather than REB therapy.

While this is the preferred REBT order and a clear rationale will be given to and discussed with the client for using this order, if the latter is adamant that they want to use a different order, then the therapist will be mindful of the working alliance (see above). As such, they will encourage the client to proceed according to their preferences and review the results of doing so at a later date. There is little to be gained and much to be lost by the therapist attempting to force a client to use the preferred REBT order when they are very reluctant to do so. Indeed, an REBT therapist who does this is likely to hold rigid ideas about how REBT must be practised and is thus being unhelpfully dogmatic!

A second area where REBT has views on the order of treatment concerns whether to deal with meta-disturbance issues before disturbance issues or vice versa. The preferred order is to deal with a meta-disturbance issue first if a) its presence interferes with the client working on the disturbance issue in or out of the session, b) it is clinically the most critical issue of the two and centrally, from a working alliance perspective, c) if the client sees the sense of doing so.

Changing Rigid and Extreme Attitudes

As outlined in the theoretical section above, REBT theory hypothesises that a client's rigid and extreme attitudes largely determine their psychological problems and of the two, rigid attitudes are at the very core of such disturbance.

It follows from this that REBT therapists target for change their clients' rigid and extreme attitudes and particularly the former as early in therapy as is feasible. Other approaches in the CBT tradition (see Wills 2008) argue that to focus on such underlying attitudes early on in therapy will create an obstacle to change because people are deemed to be reluctant to make deep-structure change in preference to surface-structure change. REBT therapists argue differently and hold that as long as clients understand the role that such rigid and extreme attitudes play in determining and maintaining their problems and appreciate that they need to examine and change these attitudes if they are to address their problems effectively, then examining their attitudes early in therapy will not pose an obstacle to change, particularly if doing so is grounded in a good working alliance between therapist and client.

Perhaps the most distinctive feature about REBT practice is the efforts that REBT therapists make to help their clients change their rigid and extreme attitudes to flexible and non-extreme attitudes, once they have identified the former and helped their clients construct the latter. This process involves several steps.

The first step in helping clients to change their rigid and extreme attitudes to their flexible and non-extreme alternatives is to assist them in detecting the former. In the first instance, this involves teaching clients about these dysfunctional attitudes and their nature. These are characterised by rigidity and by being extreme. Rigid attitudes occur most frequently in the form of demands and musts, and extreme attitudes which are derived from these rigid attitudes take the form of awfulising attitudes, attitudes of unbearability and devaluation (of self, others and life conditions) attitudes. REBT therapists use several ways to teach clients about this vital aspect of REBT theory and help them to apply this knowledge in the assessment process to detect the dysfunctional attitudes that underpin their emotional problems.

The second step to helping clients to examine and change their rigid and extreme attitudes is to encourage them to construct alternative flexible and non-extreme attitudes and encourage them to understand that holding these attitudes will help them to achieve their therapeutic goals.

As guided by REBT theory, if the therapist is targeting a rigid attitude for change (e.g. 'You must like me'), they first need to help the client to construct a flexible attitude (e.g. 'I want you to like me, but you do not have to do so'). Moreover, if the therapist is targeting an extreme attitude (i.e. an awfulising attitude, an attitude of unbearability or a devaluation attitude), they first need to help the client construct a non-extreme attitude (i.e. a non-awfulising attitude, an attitude of bearability or an unconditional acceptance attitude). Thus, if the therapist is targeting an extreme, awfulising attitude (e.g. 'It would be awful if you don't like me'), they would first help the client to construct an alternative non-extreme, non-awfulising attitude (e.g. 'It would be bad if you don't like me, but it would not be awful'). If the therapist fails to help the client construct a flexible and/or non-extreme attitude alternative to their rigid and/or extreme attitude, then they will impede the change process as the client will be in an attitude vacuum, being encouraged to give up their dysfunctional attitude, but without anything to replace it with.

The third step in helping clients to change their rigid and extreme attitudes to their flexible and non-extreme alternatives is encouraging them to discriminate their rigid and extreme attitudes from their constructed flexible and non-extreme attitudes. In the same way that REBT therapists educate their clients to understand rigid/extreme attitudes and the forms that they take, they also teach them to understand what flexible/non-extreme attitudes are and the forms that they take.

Table 1 Shared (underlined) and distinguishing components of rigid/extreme and flexible/non-extreme attitudes

Components of a Rigid/ Extreme Attitude	Components of a Flexible/ Non-Extreme Attitude
Rigid Attitude **1. *Preference*** **2. *Demand Asserted*** 'I don't want my boss to criticise me and therefore he must not do so'	**Flexible Attitude** **1. *Preference*** **2. *Demand Negated*** 'I don't want my boss to criticise me, but it does not have to be the way I want must not do so'
Awfulising Attitude **1. *Evaluation of Badness*** **2. *Awfulising*** 'It would be bad if my boss criticised me and therefore it would be the end of the world'	**Non-Awfulising Attitude** **1. *Evaluation of Badness*** **2. *Non-Awfulising*** 'It would be bad if my boss criticised me, but it would not be the end of the world'
Attitude of Unbearability **1. *Struggle*** **2. *Discomfort Intolerance*** 'It would be hard to bear if my boss criticised me, and therefore, I could not bear it'	**Attitude of Bearability** **1. *Struggle*** **2. *Discomfort Tolerance*** **3. *Worth It*** **4. *Willingness*** **5. *Going To*** 'It would be hard to bear if my boss criticised me, but I could bear it, it is worth bearing, I am willing to bear it, and I am going to do so'
Devaluation Attitude **1. *Negatively Evaluated Aspect*** **2. *Asserted Devaluation (of self/other/life)*** 'If my boss criticised me, that would be bad and would prove that I am an idiot'	**Unconditional Acceptance Attitude** **1. *Negatively Evaluated Aspect*** **2. *Negated Devaluation (of self/other/life)*** **3. *Asserted Unconditional Acceptance (of self/other/life)*** 'If my boss criticised me, that would be bad but would not prove that I am an idiot person. It would prove that I am a fallible human being capable of doing well and poorly'

A very important part of this process is helping clients to understand keenly the differences between rigid/extreme and flexible/non-extreme attitudes. Table 1 outlines clearly the full differences between these different sets of attitudes.

Examining Clients' Rigid and Extreme Attitudes and Flexible and Non-Extreme Attitudes

After REBT therapists have helped their clients to see the differences between their dysfunctional and functional attitudes, they move on to help their clients to question or examine these attitudes. Albert Ellis (1994) referred to this process as 'disputing' and which I call 'examining' here. This is done after clients understand the relationship between their rigid and extreme attitudes and their emotional problems and their flexible and non-extreme attitudes and their goals. What follows applies both to clients' specific attitudes and their more general attitudes.

As DiGiuseppe (1991) has shown, 'examining' involves questioning both clients' rigid and extreme attitudes and flexible and non-extreme attitudes to the point where they see the reasons for the dysfunctionality of the former (i.e. they are false, illogical and lead largely to poor results) and for the functionality of the latter (i.e. they are true, logical and lead largely to good results). Also, short didactic explanations are given until clients reach the same insight. These questions/explanations are directed to clients' rigid and flexible attitudes as well as to their extreme and non-extreme attitudes, and this is done using a variety of styles (see below).

In common with other CBT therapists, REBT therapists ask clients questions about the empirical status and the pragmatic status of their attitudes. However, they also ask them about the logical status of their attitudes (e.g. 'which is more logical: your attitude, "Because I want to do well, therefore I have to"; or the alternative attitude, "I do not have to do well even though I want to"?'). Other CBT therapists do this less frequently, and thus, this is a distinctive feature of REBT. It may be that empirical ('Is it true?') and pragmatic ('Is it helpful?') arguments are more persuasive to clients than logical arguments ('Is it logical?'). We do not know because the relevant research has not been done. Even if this is the case, in general, REBT therapists would still use logical questioning/disputing of attitudes for two reasons. First, they do not know, on a priori grounds, which clients will find which arguments most persuasive in changing their rigid and extreme attitudes to their flexible and non-extreme alternatives. Just because the majority of clients may find logical arguments unpersuasive, it does not follow that all will do so and to withhold such arguments from those who might find them persuasive would not be good practice. So, REBT therapists tend to use all three arguments to see, as I said above, which arguments will be most persuasive with which clients.

Second, REBT therapists use empirical, pragmatic and logical arguments while examining attitudes in order to cover all the bases (comprehensiveness). This comprehensiveness may itself be productive. Thus, even if clients find empirical and pragmatic arguments more persuasive than logical arguments, it may still be worthwhile employing such arguments in that they may add value to the overall effectiveness of the attitude examination process. Some clients may find it persuasive that their dysfunctional attitudes are false, unhealthy and logical even if they find the logical argument weak on its own.

Compromises in REBT

REBT therapists have a preferred strategy and, as we have seen, this involves encouraging clients to achieve attitude change. However, it recognises that clients may not be able or willing to change their rigid and extreme attitudes and, in such cases, it recommends making compromises with the ideal of attitude change (Dryden 1987). Thus, when a client is not able or willing to change their dysfunctional attitudes, the REBT practitioner can help them to:

1. Change their distorted inferences.
2. Change their behaviour.
3. Learn new skills.
4. Change or leave the situation in which they experience their problem.

Conclusion

REBT is the oldest of the cognitive-behaviour therapies. Perhaps partly because of this, it struggles for professional attention in a therapeutic world where the novel is often more appealing than the traditional. However, it also seems to be the case that the theory and practice are not fully understood (see Dryden 2013) and thus, in this Introduction, I have placed much emphasis on outlining and discussing REBT's main theoretical and practical features. For if a therapeutic approach is to be appropriately evaluated, it first needs to be properly understood!

Part 1

General Good Practice in REBT

Chapter 1

Explore Briefly Your Clients' Expectations of REBT and Their Previous Experiences of Therapy

When you see a client for the first time it is useful to discover what they know about REBT, what they expect from it and what their previous experiences of therapy have been. This should be done briefly. The purpose of exploring a client's knowledge and expectations of REBT is to help them to capitalise on their realistic knowledge and expectations and to correct any misconceptions they may have about REBT at the outset.

Therapist:	I practise an approach to therapy called Rational Emotive Behaviour Therapy. Have you heard of it?
Client:	Yes, I have.
Therapist:	What do you know about it?
Client:	I will tell you my problems and you will teach me how to handle them rationally.
Therapist:	What do you understand by 'rationally'?
Client:	I guess it means without emotion.
Therapist:	That's not quite how I see my role as an REBT therapist. I see my role as helping us both to understand your problems one at a time and helping you to deal constructively with the adversity at the heart of each problem.This doesn't mean that you will have no emotion. It means that your emotional response to the adversity with be healthy rather unhealthy. Does that make sense?
Client:	Yes, it does.
Therapist:	Is that the kind of help you are looking for?
Client:	Yes, it is.

DOI: 10.4324/9781003423348-3

Similarly, the purpose of finding out about a client's previous experiences of therapy is to let them know that you will be building on what they found helpful and you will be avoiding what they found unhelpful.

Therapist: You said you have had therapy before. How did you find it?

Client: I didn't like the therapy I had before because the therapist didn't say very much. I felt uncomfortable with all the silences.

Therapist: Therapy with me will be different. It will be more like a conversation, and any silences will be brief if we need to think about what has been said. How does that sound?

Client: Much better.

Key Idea

Be brief in exploring your clients' knowledge and expectations about REBT and any previous experiences they may have had. Use any opportunity to give accurate information about REBT and to put REBT into a constructive frame.

Chapter 2

Develop the Therapeutic Relationship in REBT through the Work

The therapeutic relationship is important in any approach to therapy. In REBT we argue the best way to develop a good collaborative working relationship with a client is to get down to the business of helping them as quickly as possible. We argue that in REBT you can show your client respect and acceptance, establish trust and demonstrate empathy *while* helping them by assessing and intervening with their nominated issues rather than *before* doing this. In short, in REBT, we hold that a productive relationship can be developed *through* an early problem-solving focus:

Trainee: Surely, I have to show the client that I care before working on their problems otherwise, it seems so impersonal.

Trainer: But can't you demonstrate that you care by getting down to the business of helping the client as quickly as possible?

Trainee: I suppose so, but if the client doesn't trust you how will they fully open up to you?

Trainer: Well, they may not open up to you fully straight away, but if they experience you as keen to help them as quickly as possible and you show them you are competent, wouldn't that help them to trust you and open up to you more fully?

Trainee: That's a good point. But isn't REBT on its own in saying that the therapeutic relationship is not important?

DOI: 10.4324/9781003423348-4

Trainer: REBT does not say that the therapeutic relationship is not important. It argues that it IS important, but not ALL important in therapy. We argue that problems are solved by us helping clients to by develop flexible and non-extreme attitudes towards adversities and then by doing something constructive about these adversities. The therapeutic relationship on its own can't achieve this but it can facilitate our work in this area.

Key Idea

A good therapeutic relationship in REBT is developed through helping clients rather than before helping them.

Chapter 3

Set and Keep to a Therapeutic Agenda

A therapeutic agenda is an agreement between the therapist and client concerning how they are going to use time in a session.

Set a Therapeutic Agenda

Setting such an agenda with a client at the beginning of every session helps to keep both you and your client focused on the respective tasks that need to be undertaken in order to make the optimum use of therapy time. Agenda-setting also emphasises the structured approach of REBT.

Therapist:	So, let's set our agenda for the session. I would like to begin by reviewing the homework task that we negotiated at the end of our last session. After that, what issues would you like to discuss?
Client:	I have two issues that I want to discuss. One is another example of dealing with criticism and the other is a decision I have to make about my job.
Therapist:	Which has the greatest priority for you?
Client:	The decision about my job.
Therapist:	So, shall we give most time to that?
Client:	Yes.
Therapist:	So let me suggest something. Since the example related to the homework task that you did, shall

DOI: 10.4324/9781003423348-5

	we link it to that and deal with it first, while being mindful of spending most time on your job-related decision?
Client:	I am happy with that.

In this example the therapist is responsive to the client in agreeing that they will cover both issues that the client wants to discuss. However, the therapist suggest a particular order, one that links one of the proposed issues to the homework task that they are going to review at the beginning. If the client disagreed with this suggested order the therapist would have modified the agenda to meet the client's preference, thus strengthening the working alliance between the two. Effective agenda-setting is part of the process of socialising your clients into REBT so that they realise what will be expected of them in each session.

Proficient agenda-setting takes no more than a couple of minutes, so aim for this time target, but, as Walen et al. (1992: 66) point out: 'Agenda setting is a skill that requires training, supervision and lots and lots of practice'. Agenda-setting is a flexible procedure; so, if your client comes to the session feeling suicidal or bursts into tears in the session, then this becomes the agenda for immediate discussion.

Keep to a Therapeutic Agenda

Once the therapist and client have agreed the agenda for the session, it is the therapist's job to ensure that both of them keep to the agenda unless there is a good reason to depart from it. Otherwise, the session will ramble and the client will not get as much from the session as they would if the agenda was followed.

Client:	That reminds me of another problem that I have which is related to my problem with dealing with criticism. Let me tell you about it.
Therapist:	Before you do that, let me remind you that you wanted to spend most time in the session on deciding what you want to do with your job. Is that

	still the case or do you want to change the agenda and focus on this new issue?
Client:	No, you are right. I want to talk about my job decision.

If the therapist had not checked with the client about the status of this new item, then they may well have discussed it and the client may have left dissatisfied because they had not talked about what was key to them, i.e. their job-related decision. However, sometimes the client does want to modify the agenda and that is usually fine and shows the therapist's attunement and flexibility.

Key Idea

Set an agenda in every session and then keep to it unless there is a good reason to modify it.

Chapter 4

Obtain a Problem List

Clients do not always present with one clear, discrete problem. It may happen that a number of problem areas will emerge, which may encourage some clients to feel that they are overwhelmed with problems. The importance of a problem list is stated by Fennell (1989: 179):

> Drawing up an agreed problem-list gives the patient immediate experience of cognitive behaviour therapy as a collaborative enterprise. It helps the therapist to understand the patient's perspective, and allows patients to feel that a genuine effort is being made to grasp their internal reality…[T]he problem-list also imposes order on chaos. A mass of distressing experiences is reduced to a number of relatively specific difficulties. This process of 'problem-reduction' is crucial to the encouragement of hope, since it implies the possibility of control.

There are a number of ways that the therapist can develop a problem list with a client.

- This can be done in the first session where the therapist asks the client what problems the client wants to focus on during therapy. It is important that both keep a copy of the list and add to it and subtract from it over the course of therapy.
- A start may be made in the session and the client asked to complete it as a homework task.
- The therapist may give a rationale for the development of a problem list and ask the client to compile it as a homework task, thus devoting the session to dealing with the client's nominated

DOI: 10.4324/9781003423348-6

problem (i.e. the problem that the client wishes to discuss with the therapist in the present session).

It can happen that the client lists a great deal of problems and gets overwhelmed by their sheer number. In this case, the therapist can help the client to group the items into a small number of themes. This usually helps the client to gain a sense of control and see this 'themed' list as manageable.

The problem list can be useful if a client comes to a session without any item to discuss. If this happens, the therapist can encourage the client to consult their problem list to see if there is any problem listed that needs coverage, even though the client may not be troubled by it at the time. It can also serve as a way of assessing progress with the client, for example, being asked to rate progress on each item on a ten-point scale.

Key Idea

Draw up a problem list with your clients and explain its use in REBT.

Chapter 5

Generally, Be Active and Directive

REBT therapists usually adopt an active-directive style. They are active in, among other things, asking questions, collecting assessment data, limiting client rambling or generalities, formulating hypotheses, problem defining, goal-setting, helping clients to examine attitudes and negotiating homework tasks. Through these and other activities, they direct their clients to the cognitive core (i.e. rigid and extreme attitudes) of their emotional and behavioural problems. REBT deems this approach to be more effective in helping clients change than a passive or non-directive style of intervention. I have trained REBT therapists for over 45 years and consider that being active-directive is the aspect of the therapy with which most trainees struggle. This is especially the case with trainees who have had prior training in person-centred therapy or psychodynamic therapy (Dryden 2024). While you follow a client's lead in understanding their problems from their frame of reference, when it comes to conceptualising these problems from the REBT perspective, it is important that you take the lead in doing so. Before you do the latter, it is important that you explain to your client what you are going to do and why and elicit their agreement.

Therapist:	So, you felt hurt when you were criticised unfairly by your mother and you refused to talk to her. Is that correct?
Client:	Yes.
Therapist:	Do you think that your response was constructive or unconstructive?
Client:	Definitely unconstructive.

DOI: 10.4324/9781003423348-7

Therapist: OK. What I would like to do is to put this episode into REBT's *ABC* framework and see if this can shed some light on what determined your response and what you can do about it. Does that make sense?

Client: Yes.

Therapist: OK if I take the lead then?

Client: Please do.

In my experience, most clients have no difficulties in accepting an active-directive approach once you explain the rationale for it. Clients expect some problem-solving action from you and being active-directive can usually help to bring this about in a relatively brief period of time. In order to increase your own level of active-directiveness, review your session audiotapes, engage in role plays with other trainees or colleagues, watch videos of leading REBT therapists in action and read transcripts of their therapy sessions.

In the following extract, the therapist focuses the client's attention very quickly on her guilt-inducing thinking:

Client: I feel very guilty about what I did.

Therapist: What exactly do you feel guilty about?

[Here, the therapist is asking a focused question to discover the client's adversity at A.]

Client: I slept with my husband's best friend. My husband has always been faithful to me. That's why I feel guilty, and I can't get what I did out of my mind.

Therapist: Do you think everyone would feel guilty in these circumstances?

Client: I guess not.

Therapist: Some would feel guilty and couldn't stop thinking about what they did. Some would feel guilt-free remorse and try to understand why they did what they did but without rumination. And some wouldn't care. Which response would be healthiest for you?

[Here, the therapist is outlining the client's options as a prelude to emotional goal-setting.]

Client: Definitely, the second.

Therapist: So, shall we figure out what led to your rumination-based guilt and see what we can do about it to help you feel guilt-free remorse?

Client: Yes!

[Note how the therapist takes the lead in using key aspects of REBT's ABC framework. Also, note how the therapist engages the client during the discussion. You can take an active-directive stance as an REBT therapist and still engage the client actively in the process.]

Key Idea

Take an active-directive stance in REBT but do so while engaging clients fully in the therapeutic process.

Chapter 6

Intervene in Your Clients' Problems without Knowing the 'Big Picture' First

In REBT, we hold that we can help clients with their nominated problems without obtaining a total picture of the client's past, present and future. While understanding the 'big picture' first before intervening is common practice in certain approaches to psychotherapy, doing so is not regarded as an efficient use of therapy time in REBT.

Supervisor (listening to the digital recording of the session):	The client said that he felt anxious when he is in the company of people who he thinks is better educated than him. Why did you not ask him what he was most anxious about rather than explore his educational history?
Supervisee:	I thought that exploring his educational history would offer some clues to his anxiety.
Supervisor:	I see. However, in REBT, we consider that doing an accurate *ABC* assessment would help us more efficiently to discover this client's adversity and help him deal with what he is most anxious about. You may find out his entire educational history and still not discover what he is most anxious about.
Supervisee:	But isn't getting the big picture important?
Supervisor:	You can get a better sense of the big picture as you work more with the client, but getting down to work with doing an *ABC* assessment of the client's nominated problem is more important.

DOI: 10.4324/9781003423348-8

Having made the above point, there are times when you may want to carry out what is called a case formulation (Persons 2012) before embarking upon intervention. Elsewhere, I have argued that carrying out such a formulation, referred to as a UPCP (Understanding the Person in the Context of his Problems), should be done if the 'case' is complicated or expected progress has not occurred (Dryden 1998). In the main, however, REBT therapists develop a formulation of the 'case' as they go rather than routinely before intervention.

Key Idea

Start working with specific client problems rather than getting a 'big picture' of all your client's problems first unless their problems are very complex or expected progress has not materialised.

Chapter 7

Deal with Clients' Present Problems without Getting Caught up in Their Past

In REBT, we focus on how the client unwittingly maintains their emotional problems rather than on how these problems were acquired in the first place. We argue in REBT that the therapist can understand the client's past through the lens of the present by helping the client to identify their current rigid and extreme attitudes towards these past events.

Client: I still feel miserable about my husband dumping me ten years ago. He has caused me all this misery.

[The client clearly blames her husband for her ten years of misery.]

Therapist: It is certainly unpleasant to be dumped but do you think all women who were dumped ten years ago by their husband would still be miserable?

Client: But who wants to be dumped?

Therapist: Probably no one. Some women would still be miserable, but wouldn't others have picked up the pieces of their life and moved on, perhaps finding a new partner if they wanted to?

[Here the therapist is pointing out to the client that she has options and that she is not doomed to be miserable because she was dumped ten years ago.]

Client: Yes, but how can I move on. He made me feel worthless when he dumped me. Who else would want me?

DOI: 10.4324/9781003423348-9

Therapist: Let's say that he did try to make you feel worthless. Did you agree with him or disagree with him back then?

[The therapist is helping the client to see that she is the ultimate judge of her worth.]

Client: I suppose I agreed with him
Therapist: And when you are miserable do you still agree with him?
Client: Yes.
Therapist: Is thinking of yourself as worthless why you believe that no one else would want you?

Exploring this client's past will probably prolong her present distress; so, the crucial thing is for the client to give up her currently held ideas so that tomorrow's existence can be better than yesterday's. 'In a sense, the person each day chooses to either hold onto disturbed beliefs or to give them up' (Grieger and Boyd 1980: 76–7).

Some clients will be preoccupied with past events and want to talk about them to make sense of them. These events will often need to be explored before such clients can focus on their present difficulties (looking back is not contra-indicated in REBT as long as you do not dwell there). This historical quest will involve you helping your clients to uncover their past attitudes towards past events. However, as an REBT therapist you will also want to help the client see that they may well currently hold these attitudes, and if they want to deal with their current disturbed feelings, they need to examine the attitudes that underpin their disturbance.

Key Idea

Explore your clients' disturbed feelings about past events through the lens of their current rigid and extreme attitudes. However, there may be times when you need to uncover their past attitudes towards past events. If so, do so, but look for ways of linking past and currently held rigid and extreme attitudes.

Chapter 8

Help Your Clients to Express Themselves through the REBT's *ABC* Framework

When clients start therapy, they understandably want to talk about their problems in their own way. That is fine at the outset; they should be free to express themselves in their own way and, after all, an alternative framework for their self-exploration has not yet been offered to them. Once you start teaching your clients about REBT, it is important to encourage them to shift from unstructured to structured self-exploration through the use of the *ABC* framework.

Compare the following two scenarios. In the first, the therapist is working with the client's own mode of self-expression, while in the second, the therapist uses the *ABC* framework to facilitate client self-exploration.

Client: I really am struggling to be open with my girlfriend at the moment. I want to but it's a struggle.
Therapist: What's the struggle about?
Client: Part of me wants to, but another part of me is holding back.
Therapist: So, you are torn and can't decide what to do in practice.
Client: Yes.

[While this therapist communicates their understanding of the client's struggle, working with the way that the client is expressing themself is not moving the therapeutic conversation forward.]

Client: I really am struggling to be open with my girlfriend at the moment. I want to but it's a struggle.
Therapist: What's the feeling that is holding you back?

DOI: 10.4324/9781003423348-10

[Here, the therapist is using the C in the ABC framework to identify the obstacle.]

Client: Anxiety.
Therapist: And what are you most anxious about with respect to being open with your girlfriend?

[Here, the therapist is using the A in the ABC framework to identify the client's adversity.]

Client: That she will ridicule me.
Therapist: So, part of you wants to be open with your girlfriend but there is another part that is anxious about doing so in case she ridicules you. Is that right?
Client: That is exactly right.

In the second scenario, by using REBT's *ABC* framework, the therapist helps the client to be understood at a deeper level than in the first scenario.

Key Idea

Whenever possible, encourage your clients to express themselves in a structured way using REBT's *ABC* framework.

Chapter 9

Listen Actively

You might believe you are actively listening to your clients' problems because you are nodding your head, producing a string of 'hmms'; or using seemingly empathic words such as 'sure', 'right' or 'absolutely'; and employing paraphrasing, reflecting and summarising as part of your listening skills. I would suggest that, in REBT terms, this is passive, not active, listening. Active listening in REBT is being on the alert for the *ABC* components of clients' presenting problems as shown in Chapter 8. This 'search for the ABCs of client problems begins the moment the person enters therapy' (Grieger and Boyd 1980: 59).

Compare the following two scenarios. In the first, the trainee is *not* listening for the *ABC* components, while in the second, the trainee does do so.

Client:	I mean it's always the same. My boss always leaves it to the last minute before giving me a whole load of work so I have to stay late.
Trainee:	Your boss seems to be taking advantage of you.
Client:	You can say that again he treats a lot of people as if they are objects, not people.
Trainee:	Mm-hmm
Client:	Here is another example

[While the client may feel that this trainee is on their side, by passive listening, the trainee is encouraging the client to come up with more examples of the boss's bad behaviour. This is not the task of therapy.]

DOI: 10.4324/9781003423348-11

Client: I mean it's always the same. My boss always leaves it to the last minute before giving me a whole load of work so I have to stay late.
Trainee: How do you feel when he does this?

[Here, the trainee is using the C in the ABC framework to identify the client's feeling.]

Client: As mad as hell.
Trainee: Do you say anything when he leaves things to the last minute before giving you this work?
Client: No.
Trainee: Do you want to say something?

[Here, the trainee is asking for the client's goal.]

Client: Yes, I do.
Trainee: What stops you?
Client: I'm so mad that I think I will say something to him that I may regret.
Trainee: So, if I helped you deal with your mad feeling would that help you to say something when he gives you that late work?
Client: Yes, it would.

[Here, through active listening and responding on the basis of such listening, the therapist helps the client to create a focus for the rest of the session.]

Therapist: OK, let's do that. What are you so mad about when he leaves it to the last minute to give you work?

[Here, the trainee is using the A in the ABC framework to identify what the client is most mad about.]

Cormier and Cormier (1985: 89) define listening 'as involving three processes: receiving a message, processing a message, and sending a message'. In REBT terms, receiving a message is your clients' account of their problems, processing the message is assembling an *ABC* structure of their problems in your mind, and sending a message is presenting this structure to your clients for their consideration and comment. Active listening requires your sustained concentration and direct questioning in each and every session with the purpose of maintaining the focus on helping clients with their nominated emotional problems. Passive listening is more of an invitation to let your thoughts or your clients' thoughts wander away from an agreed focus if that is where the exploration leads.

Key Idea

Listen actively, not passively, to your clients' problems and use REBT's *ABC* framework to guide your active listening.

Chapter 10

Ensure that Your Clients Answer the Questions You Have Asked

When you ask a question, you presumably want an answer. REBT therapists ask direct questions in order to elicit specific information from their clients (e.g. 'How did you feel when you did not get the promotion?' or 'What were you thinking when you made that mistake in front of your colleagues?'). When a client does not answer an important question, it is good practice to draw this tactfully to the client's attention and ask the question again until you get an answer.

Therapist: This seems important. How did you feel when you were overlooked for promotion again?

Client: I thought that perhaps, I wasn't trying hard enough and next year I will have to try harder.

[Here, the client hasn't answered the therapist's question about their feelings about being overlooked for promotion again. The therapist has noticed this and goes back to their question.]

Therapist: Maybe, but how did you feel about being overlooked again this time?

Client: Oh, I see. I felt hurt.

Your clients will frequently give you thoughts when you ask them for feelings. These cognitions are usually prefaced by the words 'I feel' and thereby create the impression that your questions have been answered. This is not the case. You are looking for an unhealthy negative emotion (e.g. depression, anger, guilt) connected to your client's adversity at *A*.

DOI: 10.4324/9781003423348-12

Therapist: How did you feel when your husband shouted at you?

Client: I felt that this was the end of our marriage.

Therapist: That was a thought, not a feeling. How did you feel?

Client: I felt everything I worked for was in ruins.

Therapist: OK. You are giving me thoughts and we will examine those presently. Now feelings or emotions are usually expressed in one word like 'anger' or 'anxiety'. More than one word is usually a thought. So how did you feel in your gut when your husband shouted at you?

[The therapist explains a distinction between thoughts and feelings as part of their attempt to get an answer to their question. The therapist uses the evocative term 'in your gut' as further encouragement to revel the client's feelings.]

Client: Very anxious.

Clients often respond to questions with 'I don't know'. You may wonder how you are supposed to obtain answers to this reply. If you accept such replies without further enquiry, this will help to maintain clients' ignorance about their problems instead of promoting insight into them. In this dialogue excerpt, the therapist uses REBT theory to help the client.

Therapist: So, you felt hurt when your friend forgot your birthday. What were you hurt about?

Client: I don't know.

Therapist: You said, 'I don't know' very quickly. Take your time to think about the question, 'What were you hurt about when your friend forgot your birthday'?

Client (long pause): I don't know.

Therapist: Would you like some help here?

Client: Yes, please.

Therapist: Well, when people feel hurt, they may feel hurt about the other person treating them unfairly, or in an uncaring way…

Client: That's it, I thought that my friend doesn't care about me.

When a client says, 'I don't know' see it as a challenge, rather than as a block, in order to bring the information, which is currently outside of your client's awareness, into your client's awareness. Asking questions is not a form of interrogation that is supposed to put your clients on the defensive, but a means of stimulating greater introspective awareness of their disturbance-inducing patterns of thinking.

Key Idea

When your clients have not answered your questions, bring this to their attention and help them in a variety of ways to answer these questions.

Chapter 11

Interrupt Clients When They Ramble or Talk Too Much

REBT views interrupting clients when they meander or are verbose as necessary rather than impolite. However, it is important to ensure that you explain the reasons for your interruptions and ask for their permission to do so. Only some aspects of what clients talk about is clinically significant from an REBT perspective. When you remain silent then they may think that everything they say is significant and you want to hear all of it. Valuable therapy time can be wasted through not reining in your clients when they are overly talkative or ramble.

Here is a good example of how to do this which I suggest you do at the beginning of therapy with all clients so that they have a rationale for being interrupted, give their permission for you to do so and indicate how you can best do this.

Therapist: Before we focus on the problem that you want to deal with, first I need to ask you something. Is that OK?

Client: Sure.

Therapist: Well, it may happen that once we have agreed on a particular focus that you may inadvertently depart from it. If so, is it OK if I interrupt you when this happens?

Client: Definitely.

Therapist: I may need to interrupt you if you give me more information that I may need in order to help you. Is it OK if I interrupt you if this happens.

DOI: 10.4324/9781003423348-13

Client: Yes.
Therapist: Thank you. Now, how best can I interrupt you?
Client: Just cut in and say, 'May I interrupt you?'

You may be reluctant to interrupt your clients even if they have given you the go ahead because you fear that by doing so you will negatively impact the therapeutic relationship. Treat your fears as hypotheses to be tested. If some clients do become upset when you interrupt them, elicit their thoughts (e.g. 'I feel you're not really interested in me. I'm just another head case to deal with') and show them that it is their appraisals of the interruptions that lead to their upset feelings, not the interruption itself (though interrupting insensitively contributes to the client being upset).

Trainees often say that one of the major reasons they do not interrupt clients who are verbose is because they are not sure when to (e.g. 'How do I know whether the client is giving me too much information or going off at a tangent?'). We would suggest a simple rule of thumb to help you with these clients: are you able to make *ABC* sense from what your client is saying? If not, interrupt to clarify and put what the client said into the *ABC* format.

Key Idea

Clients may stray from the focus you have agreed with them, or they may give you far too much information. Asking clients at the outset for permission to interrupt them under these conditions and receiving such permission enables you to interrupt them in practice and be time efficient in your therapeutic work.

Chapter 12

Be Clear and Concise in What You Say to Clients

In the previous chapter, I argued that it is important that you interrupt a client if they are being verbose. It is also important that you are clear and concise in your practice of REBT since if you are verbose and obtuse then your client may feel confused by your lack of clarity or overwhelmed by the amount you talk.

Over the years, I have supervised many REBT therapists, and the effective ones are those who are clear and concise in what they say. If they do have to talk at length, for example, when teaching a complex REBT concept, they 'chunk' the amount of information they give the client and periodically ask the client to put into their own words what they (the client) think that they (the therapist) has been saying.

Your clients' ability to think through their problems and solutions to them usually varies in inverse ratio to the amount of talking that you do and the clarity with which you talk. The more talking you do and the vaguer you are, the less time they will spend on examining the rigid and extreme attitudes that underpin their problems, for example.

Trainee therapists' lack of clarity and verbosity can also stem from anxiety: your demand to 'get it right' every time you open your mouth, i.e. your questions and comments must have textbook precision. Instead of refining each question or comment in the light of your clients' responses, you attempt to refine it too much before offering it to your clients, thereby baffling them and often yourself as well. I advise you to practise clarity and verbal economy and i) give short clear statements and ii) ask short questions, one at a time. You may be surprised how often your clients now understand what you have said to them and what you have asked them.

DOI: 10.4324/9781003423348-14

As an exercise, record some of your therapy session and listen to them for instances where you were unclear and/or verbose. Formulate much shorter and clearer statements or questions which you could have said instead.

Key Idea

Make your communications with your clients concise, clear and direct.

Chapter 13

Obtain Feedback from Your Clients

Feedback enables you to determine your clients' level of understanding of and agreement with REBT concepts, their progress and stumbling blocks, their reactions to therapy and the therapist. Obtaining this information is part of REBT's open and collaborative approach to problem solving. Not obtaining feedback suggests that your clients' views are unimportant and can turn them into passive (and possibly resentful) partners in therapy. Feedback from clients requires them providing specific information. Giving nods and making paraverbal responses, one-word replies or general comments are valueless.

Therapist: I've been explaining how REBT sees the differences between unconditional self-acceptance and self-esteem. Do you understand the differences?

Client: Yeah.

[As 'Yeah' could mean several things it is a starting point for clarification.]

Therapist: I'm not sure what 'Yeah' means. Could you explain what these differences are?

Client: Well, self-acceptance is about not putting yourself down under any circumstances, while with self-esteem you're more likely to put yourself down when things go against you.

[As understanding is not synonymous with agreement or indicating usefulness, further feedback needs to be sought.]

Therapist: That's a good way of putting it. Do you think that self-acceptance could be more helpful to you than self-esteem?

DOI: 10.4324/9781003423348-15

Client (shrugs shoulders):	I guess.

[The client's response suggests that the therapist needs to elicit more information.]

Therapist:	What does that mean?
Client:	Well, it's all right being self-accepting, but you still want to get on in life. Self-acceptance sounds like you just sit around all day saying, 'I can accept myself', but so what? Big deal. At least with self-esteem, you're pushing yourself to succeed, make something of yourself.

[Feedback has revealed the client's misunderstanding of self-acceptance and presented the therapist with an opportunity to correct it.]

Therapist:	Thanks for the feedback. That's not what I mean by self-acceptance. I may not have explained it very clearly. Let me try again. Self-acceptance is the basis for striving to reach your goals in life but without condemning yourself when you encounter setbacks or failures along the way. Has that made it clearer?
Client:	I like the way you've explained it now. The picture of self-acceptance will be helpful. It will help me strive for my goals without condemning myself if I hit snags along the way. It's not about being passive.

[The client's motivation for change based on self-acceptance has been activated.]

The same process applies to end-of-session feedback: when you ask, 'What was helpful and unhelpful about today's session?', ensure that your clients' responses are clear and specific.

Key Idea

Obtain clear and concrete feedback from your clients on a regular basis.

Chapter 14

Confront Your Clients, But Do So with Tact, Respect, Warmth and Care

Confrontation can be seen as in-your-face aggression, arguing, power struggles and general nastiness towards someone else. In REBT, confrontation means acting assertively when the therapist detects discrepancies between, for example:

- What a client is saying and what they have said before.
- What a client says and what they do.
- What a client is communicating verbally and nonverbally.
- The way a client views their problem and the way the therapist views it.

'Confrontation in counseling is particularly encouraged when the therapist notes discrepancies in the client's thoughts, feelings, and actions' (Walen et al. 1992: 61).

Novice therapists often avoid confrontation because, among other reasons, they see it (wrongly) as a form of bullying, they prefer to seek comfort in therapy or they believe confrontation will lead to some perceived catastrophe (e.g. the client storming out of the room). Confrontation brings to the client's attention issues that need addressing. Effective REBT therapists will do this directly, but with tact and respect for the client. They will also give a rationale for the confrontation and will ask for permission to confront the client before doing so (see Dryden 2024).

Therapist:	Sometimes a therapist needs to day something that a client may find difficult to hear.
Client:	OK.
Therapist:	I would like to do this now, but want your permission to do so.

DOI: 10.4324/9781003423348-16

Client: OK, go ahead.

Therapist: Well, You say you want to save your relationship, but then you tell me that you are going on dating sites. There seems to be a discrepancy between what you are saying and what you are doing in this area that I would like to understand.

Because the term 'confrontation' can have negative connotations as discussed at the beginning of this chapter, I recommend that therapists don't use this term with clients. I recommend the more descriptive, 'There seems to be a discrepancy between what you say and what you are doing on this issue, that I would like to understand'. Tactful, respectful communication facilitates the therapeutic relationship. However, it is important for the therapist to get feedback on this point after 'confronting' the client.

Therapist: How did you feel after I brought to your attention what I saw as a discrepancy between what you were saying about saving your relationship and your behaviour in going on dating sites?

Client: It was an issue that needed to be brought out into the open.

Therapist: What effect has it had on our working relationship?

Client: A positive one because I can rely on you to challenge me, but you did it without being harsh. I felt you were on my side.

The client's last point is important. When 'confronting' a client it is important you do this with tact, respect, warmth and care so that the client does experience you as on their side (Young 2024).

Key Idea

It is important that you 'confront' clients with important discrepancies and contradictions in their presentation. Do so with directness but with tact, respect, warmth and care so that you are experienced as being on the side of your clients.

Chapter 15

Work Collaboratively with Your Clients

REBT stresses collaboration: therapist and client working together to tackle the latter's problem. This involves you doing the following:

- Ensuring that the client understands and is willing to commit their active participation in the therapy process and what they are and are not responsible for.
- Ensuring that the client understands your active participation in the therapy process and what you are and are not responsible for and agrees to go forward on the basis of that understanding.
- Working with the client's nominated problem rather than one that you have decided is the most important one for the client to deal with.
- Setting a goal that is important for the client to achieve rather than one that you deem to be important for the client to work towards.
- Incorporating your client's strengths into their treatment programme rather than assume that they don't have any.
- Incorporating any past helpful strategies that the client has initiated rather than assume again that they have not done so.
- Integrating your client's view of their problems with your REBT-informed view of their problems rather than disregarding their view.
- Recognising that REBT is a useful means to an end – the client dealing effectively with their problem. It is not an end in itself.
- Taking great care that you explain the REBT framework for understanding and dealing with your client's problems in ways that they can fully understand and sign up to.
- Giving your client every opportunity to raise their doubts, reservations and objections (DROs) about any aspect of the REBT process so that you can have an open discussion of them.

DOI: 10.4324/9781003423348-17

- Spending sufficient time in the homework-task negotiation process to maximise the chances that the client will complete tasks that they have agreed to do.
- Beginning sessions with reviewing what the client did (and did not to) with respect to the homework task negotiated at the end of the previous session.
- Working with the client to identify and deal with the various obstacles to therapeutic change that may emerge during the therapeutic process.
- Working with the client to encourage them to be their own therapist by the end of the therapy process.

Key Idea

Initiate and maintain a collaborative relationship with your clients throughout the REBT process.

Chapter 16

Adopt and Maintain a Problem-Orientated Focus with Your Clients

A problem-orientated focus means not only asking for a problem and then working on it, but also dealing with any difficulty that arises in therapy. A problem-orientated outlook should be your natural stance in REBT.

Client:	Why did you look at your watch. Am I boring you?
Therapist:	I simply looked at my watch to see how much time we had left. Obviously you see it differently. But can we look at this therapeutically?
Client:	OK.
Therapist:	We have been talking about your fear of boring other people and we have seen that your underlying attitude is, 'I must be thoroughly interesting and it's terrible if I'm not'. Is that right?
Client:	Correct. So are you saying that I interpreted your behaviour as you being bored by me as a result of that attitude?
Therapist:	That is one suggestion. The other is that I was bored. Have you had the thought before that I am bored working with you?
Client:	No. I see what you mean.
Therapist:	Do you want to hear my take on what happened?
Client:	Yes, please.
Therapist:	When you hold an underlying attitude such as, 'I must be thoroughly interesting and it's terrible if I'm not', it makes you very sensitive to signs in other people that they are bored with you. So, me

DOI: 10.4324/9781003423348-18

looking at my watch led you to think I was bored with you because your underlying attitude was activated. Does that make sense?

Client: Yes it does.

Therapist: So, when you think others are bored with you, as well as looking for the evidence to support or reject that inference, you can ask yourself if your attitude that we have been working on has been activated and you can stand back and examine it as we have been doing. What do you think?

Client: That's very helpful.

[In this episode, the therapist adopts a problem-orientated stance to something that could be threatening to the working alliance. Rather than reassuring the client that the therapist is not bored, the latter uses the incident therapeutically and helps the client understand the reason for their inference and ways of dealing with it both at the level of inference and at the level of attitude.]

Key Idea

It is important for therapists to adopt and maintain a problem-orientated focus throughout the process of REBT.

Chapter 17

Keep Your Clients on Track

Your clients might view therapy as an extension of their everyday conversations, shooting off in all directions as the mood takes them. Indeed, such verbal behaviour is expected from clients (as well as the rest of us). In REBT, the talk needs to be structured and focused, if progress is to be made with the client's nominated problem. As discussed in Chapter 11, it is important to interrupt clients tactfully if they meander or are verbose.

In the following two excerpts, we can see how two trainees handled the same event.

Excerpt 1

Trainee: You say you have an explosive temper. Can you give me an example?

Client: Yesterday. My boss cancelled a meeting at the last minute. I went wild. My wife says that if I don't get my anger under control, I'm going to end up in prison, seriously ill or dead. I know she is right, but it's hard to change my behaviour.

Trainee: I think your wife has a point. Shall we explore how anger is linked to illness?

[In this excerpt, the client leaves the track, and the trainee follows him. The trainee does not bring the client back to the example of their explosive anger in order to do an ABC assessment of it. How anger is linked to illness may be an interesting issue to explore, but not at this point.]

DOI: 10.4324/9781003423348-19

Excerpt 2

Trainee: You say you have an explosive temper. Can you give me an example?

Client: Yesterday. My boss cancelled a meeting at the last minute. I went wild. My wife says that if I don't get my anger under control, I'm going to end up in prison, seriously ill or dead. I know she is right, but it's hard to change my behaviour.

Trainee: I think your wife may have a point. However, let's stick to the example you have given and understand it by using REBT's *ABC* framework.

[In this excerpt, the trainee acknowledges the client's wife's point, but gets back to the issue of assessing the client's anger.]

When your client goes off track, it may be useful sometimes to examine the clinical relevance of the new information presented in order to determine whether to stay with the present issue or discuss this new information (e.g. a client feels ashamed when discussing her panic attacks and becomes preoccupied with these shameful feelings; at this point, the clinical focus is switched from panic to shame as further progress with the former problem cannot be made until the latter one is addressed).

Key Idea

Keep your clients on track (i.e. problem-focused) when discussing their problems.

Chapter 18

Explain REBT Terminology to Your Clients and Check Their Understanding of Your Explanations

REBT has its own specialist terminology, which needs to be explained to your clients, a non-specialist group. Such terms would include 'rigid and flexible attitudes', 'awfulising', 'emotional and therapeutic responsibility' and 'unhealthy and healthy negative emotions'. You can view REBT terms as *As* that clients may misinterpret because they have their own meanings of these terms (Dryden and Yankura 1995). So you might be using the same word but in very different ways. It is, therefore, important for you to explain what you mean when you use REBT terminology with your clients and you ask them to explain what they mean when they use terms that are related to REBT theory.

As I explained in the introduction to this book, my own preferences in writing about and practising REBT is to avoid using the terms 'rational' and 'irrational', preferring the terms 'flexible and non-extreme' and 'rigid and extreme' respectively. However, given that most REBT therapists do use the terms 'rational' and irrational' with their clients, I will feature these in this chapter.

In the following excerpt, the trainee therapist begins by using the term 'irrationally' but does not explain what they mean. Note that the client responds negatively to this term because they think it means something different from how the term is used in REBT. The therapist redeems the situation by explaining what they meant.

Trainee: You're thinking irrationally when you say that your daughter should come home at the time you stated.

[Here, the trainee uses the unqualified should which I will discuss in Chapter 43.]

DOI: 10.4324/9781003423348-20

Client: How am I thinking irrationally? Am I really being unbalanced because I want my daughter to come home at a reasonable time?

[The client has interpreted 'irrationally' as 'being unbalanced'.]

Trainee: Sorry, I wasn't being clear. When I use the term 'irrational' I mean that your view of the situation – what you believe what your daughter must do – does not conform with the actual facts: she doesn't come home at the time you state. There's a mismatch between your demand and the reality. Can you explain in your own words what I mean by 'irrational'?

Client: Well my view of how it must be is not the way they are in reality. So irrational does not mean unbalanced?

Therapist: Not at all.

Client: Phew, that's a relief.

Other REBT terms that are commonly misunderstood by clients include 'self-acceptance' (e.g. some clients think that this means encouraging passivity, complacency and selfishness, and not striving for life goals), 'rational' (e.g. some clients think that this means being emotionless, cold, aloof, icily detached, always logical) and 'high frustration tolerance' (e.g. some clients think that this means maintaining a stiff upper lip at all times). Checking that your clients understand REBT terms correctly is not a one-off procedure but needs your attention throughout the course of therapy (for how to correct misconceptions about REBT, see Dryden 2024).

Key Idea

When you use REBT terminology, explain what these terms mean, then elicit from your clients their understanding of your explanation of these terms.

Chapter 19

Develop a Shared Vocabulary with Your Clients

Some clients may find REBT terminology not to their particular taste and will want to use their own personally meaningful terms. This is fine, as long as their terms reflect REBT concepts – a crucial point. Effective REBT therapists encourage their clients to use terms that reflect REBT concepts but are personally meaningful to the clients themselves. One of my clients did not resonate with the term discomfort tolerance, preferring the phrase 'suck it up' which to her meant the same as being able to tolerate discomfort but reflected her own use of language.

In the following dialogue, the therapist has explained the REBT distinction between unhealthy and healthy negative emotions (e.g. anxiety vs. concern respectively). The client prefers to use her own term, 'confident', as a healthy alternative to anxiety.

Client: Rather than feeling anxious about running workshops, I want to feel confident about doing so.

Therapist: What does feeling confident mean for you in this context?

Client: It means things going really well and I can answer all questions and knowing that I will give a good performance.

Therapist: What about if you don't do well and there are questions you can't answer? How would you feel about that?

Client: Anxious

Therapist: What would you call an alternative emotion to anxiety where you acknowledged that you might

DOI: 10.4324/9781003423348-21

	not always do well and there may be questions you can't answer, but you would not be anxious about it?
Client:	You called that concern, didn't you, but I don't like that word. I would call it 'taking things in my stride'.
Therapist:	OK, let's use 'taking things in your stride' as a healthy alternative to anxiety.

[Although 'taking things in my stride' is not an emotion, this therapist is flexible and uses this phrase as a synonym for concern. The therapist and client have developed a shared use of language to represent the healthy alternative to anxiety.]

Key Idea

Ensure that whatever terms are negotiated between you and your clients that they reflect REBT concepts.

Chapter 20

Use *B-C* Language Yourself While Teaching *B-C* Thinking to Your Clients

Clients use *A-C* language when describing their problems (e.g. 'My partner makes me angry when he ignores me'), while your task is to teach *B-C* thinking (e.g. 'I make myself angry when my partner ignores me'). It is likely that *B-C* thinking is alien to many clients but it is vital for them to adopt if they want to develop greater emotional stability in their lives.

When first learning REBT, trainees struggle to use *B-C* language when striving to teach *B-C* thinking to their clients. One way this is manifest is in the questions therapists ask their clients. Here is a list of *A-C* questions and alternatives that avoid such language. Note that the former posit causation between *A* and *C* (*A* causes *C*) while the latter posit correlation (when *A* happens, *C* happens).

Questions that Use *A-C* Language	Questions that Avoid *A-C* Language
• How did that make you feel?	• How did you feel about that?
• Did that make you feel anxious?	• Did you feel anxious about that?
• What aspect of that situation made you feel jealous?	• What did you feel most jealous about in that situation
• When he criticised you in front of your colleagues did that make you feel mad?	• Did you feel mad when he criticised you in front of your colleagues

You may struggle with *B-C* thinking for some of the following reasons: you still have reservations about emotional responsibility (can it apply in all cases?); you used *A-C* language a lot before studying

DOI: 10.4324/9781003423348-22

REBT (along with the majority of the population) and find that it is a hard habit to break.

In the following excerpt, the therapist ensures that their interventions reinforce REBT's position that *B* primarily determines *C*, not *A*.

Therapist: What are you anxious about when you meet new people?
Client: They make me anxious.
Therapist: Do you think meeting new people makes you anxious or do you think your anxiety is based on the attitudes you hold towards meeting new people?
Client: Put like that, I guess it's the attitudes I hold.
Therapist: That's right. So what do we have to discover if I am to help you with your anxiety?
Client: What my attitudes are that lead to my anxiety.

When you become adept at using *B-C* language, show some restraint in not correcting your clients every time they use *A-C* language, as this can come across as nit-picking or pedantic. Select for correction clients' *A-C* statements that are central to their emotional problems.

Key Idea

Strive to only use *B-C* language with your clients. However, do not be overly zealous in correcting them every time they lapse into *A-C* language.

Chapter 21

Socialise Your Clients into REBT in the First or Early Sessions of Therapy

Socialising your clients into REBT means letting them know what is expected of them in this form of therapy. What is expected of them includes nominating a problem, goal-setting, collaborating with the therapist on the problem-solving process, accepting emotional and therapeutic responsibility, understanding the crucial role of attitudes in determining their emotional reactions to events, examining their rigid/extreme and flexible/non-extreme attitudes and carrying out homework tasks. This socialisation process also requires you to inform your clients of your tasks. When you prepare your clients to understand REBT and the roles that you and they have to play in the therapy process, they will make more effective use of therapy (Dryden and Neenan 2021).

Therapist: I practise a form of therapy known as Rational Emotive Behaviour Therapy or REBT. It is a major approach in the field of Cognitive Behaviour Therapy. Do you know much about it?

Client: Nothing much. My cousin mentioned it when she suggested I see you.

Therapist: Well, it is a structured approach to therapy, and there is quite a bit for you to do as a client. Do you mind that?

Client: No. I have had the type of therapy when you come every week and just talk and it didn't help me much.

DOI: 10.4324/9781003423348-23

Therapist: Good. The talk needs to be focused on obtaining information that I need in order to understand your problems in REBT terms. We work together on tackling your problems. You have your tasks to carry out, and I have mine. Let me outline these tasks as I see them.

Explaining to clients at the outset of REBT what tasks they will be required to execute allows them to make an informed decision about whether or not to proceed with this form of therapy. Before this decision, people are applicants for help; after it, having chosen to proceed, they become clients. Socialisation is part of informing clients about REBT as an effective treatment for psychological disorders so that they can consent to having this treatment.

Key Idea

Let clients know what REBT is and what it calls upon you both to do. In this way, clients can be said to have given their informed consent to proceed with REBT.

Chapter 22

Teach the *ABC* Framework in a Clear Way

REBT's *ABC* framework teaches clients that they are largely responsible for disturbing themselves through the rigid and extreme attitudes they hold towards life's adversities. Clients who fail to grasp this essential principle may continue to blame others or events for their emotional problems and become bewildered when you examine them to examine their attitudes. Therefore, it is of paramount importance that you teach the *ABC* framework in a clear way if these difficulties are to be avoided.

In the following excerpt, the therapist is careful to keep the client in step with him as he teaches the model:

Therapist (writing on the whiteboard): In the framework, *A* stands for adversity or what you are most disturbed about in the problem-related situation. Let's use the example of two men wanting to go out with the same woman and she rejects both of them at *A*. Now, *B*, stands for 'basic attitudes'. The first man holds the attitude that being rejected is unfortunate but not terrible. The second man holds the attitude that it is terrible to be rejected. Now, *C* stands for the consequences of the basic attitudes. What emotions do you think the first man has about being rejected?

Client: The first man who holds the attitude that it is bad but not terrible to be rejected will be sad, but I don't think he will be depressed. The second man, on the other hand, will feel depressed.

DOI: 10.4324/9781003423348-24

Therapist: And what explains their different emotional responses?

Client: That they hold different attitudes towards being rejected.

Therapist: So, what's the major takeaway that the *ABC* framework teaches?

Client: That it's not the adversities we face that explain our emotions, it's the attitudes that we hold towards these adversities.

Therapist: That's right. In REBT, we pay a good deal of attention to the attitudes people hold towards life's adversities that explain their emotional problems. Let's see how this framework can be applied to your problems.

[This therapist chose to contrast awfulising and non-awfulising attitudes in teaching the ABC framework. You can, of course, use one or more of the four attitudes reviewed in the introduction while teaching clients this framework.]

[Here is how another therapist chose to teach this framework.]

Therapist (writing on the whiteboard): Now *A* in this model stands for adversity or the aspect of the situation that the person is most disturbed about. Two men are rejected by the woman they both want to go out with. Now at *B* which stands for basic attitudes, the first man holds a flexible and non-extreme attitude towards being rejected: 'I really wanted to go out with her, but there is no reason why she must not reject me. I will not reject myself just because she has rejected me.' The second man holds a rigid and extreme attitude at *B* towards being rejected: 'I really wanted to go out with her and therefore she absolutely should not have rejected me. Her rejection proves I am worthless'. How will both men feel about being rejected at *C* which stands for the consequences of holding basic attitudes at *B*?

Client: The first man would be sad about it but wouldn't be depressed. The second man would be depressed.

Therapist: Right. What led to their different responses?

Client: They hold different attitudes towards being rejected. The second man is rigid about the adversity and thinks it proves they are worthless. The first man is flexible about it and as he says he isn't going to reject himself.

Therapist: So, what's the major takeaway that the *ABC* framework teaches?

Client: That it's not the adversities we face that explain our emotions, it's the attitudes that we hold towards these adversities.

Therapist: That's right. In REBT, we pay a good deal of attention to the attitudes people hold towards life's adversities that explain their emotional problems. Let's see how this model can be applied to your problems.

Key Idea

Remember the *ABC* of teaching the *ABCs* of REBT: *A*lways *B*e *C*lear in your presentation of the framework.

Chapter 23

Use Socratic Dialogue and Didactic Explanations to Teach REBT Concepts to Clients Who Will Benefit the Most from Each

Socratic dialogue and didactic explanations are used to teach REBT concepts to clients. Some didactic explanation is inevitable (e.g. presenting REBT to clients), but the preferred method of client learning is through Socratic dialogue (i.e. encouraging your clients to grasp REBT principles). However, it is important to gauge which one of these teaching techniques is being profitably employed at any given moment in therapy.

It is not easy to judge whether you should use Socratic dialogue or didactic explanations with a given client. A useful rule of thumb is to begin by engaging the client in a Socratic dialogue and then if they don't respond after a proper trial then switch to providing didactic explanations. Another way is to explain the two approaches to a given client and ask them which approach they would best respond to.

With regard to didactic explanations, Grieger and Boyd (1980: 116) make an excellent point: 'Do only as much lecturing/telling as necessary to induce clients to do their own thinking'. When you are being didactic, present your explanations in small, digestible chunks instead of large indigestible slabs and, as always, check your clients' understanding 'after a brief explanation or at points during a complex explanation' (Wessler and Wessler 1980: 178).

Here is a good example of how a therapist used Socratic dialogue with a client who responded well to it.

Client:	You mentioned unconditional self-acceptance. I'm not sure what that means.
Therapist:	Would you mind if I helped you to understand this concept by asking you a series of questions?

DOI: 10.4324/9781003423348-25

[Note that the therapist does not begin engaging the client in a Socratic dialogue until they have explained what they plan to do and asked for permission to proceed.]

Client: That's fine.

Therapist: OK. Let's start with the 'self' which in this case represents you. Now we will start with the obvious. Are you human?

Client: For sure.

Therapist: Are you a complex organism or a simple one?

Client: Complex.

Therapist: Are you fallible, meaning do you make mistakes or are you infallible, meaning that you can't make mistakes?

Client: I'm definitely fallible.

Therapist: Are you static, meaning that you won't change or are you fluid, meaning that you are always changing as a person?

Client: I am fluid.

Therapist: Finally, are you unique as a human being or not?

Client: I am unique.

Therapist: To sum up you have agreed that you are a unique, fallible human being who is complex and fluid. Is that right?

Client: Yes.

Therapist: So that is you or your 'self'. Now let's look at the term unconditional.

Client: OK.

Therapist: We have concluded that you are a unique, fallible human being who is complex and fluid. Are there any conditions where that statement about you would not be true?

Client: Not that I can see.

Therapist: So you are unconditionally a unique, fallible human being who is complex and fluid. Now. Let's look at the term 'acceptance'. What do you think it means when we say unconditional self-acceptance?

Client: It seems to mean acknowledge as being true.

Therapist: That's an excellent point. So in your own words what does 'unconditional self-acceptance' mean?

Client: In my case, it means that I acknowledge that it is true that I am a unique, fallible human being who is complex and fluid and that this is unconditionally the case. What about self-esteem? Is there a place for that in REBT?

[The therapist then discusses the differences between self-esteem and unconditional self-acceptance with the client but does so knowing that the client has an accurate understanding of the REBT concept of unconditional self-acceptance.]

Finally, it is worth bearing in mind that even when primarily using Socratic dialogue to 'teach' a client an REBT concept there may be occasions when you need to supplement this with brief didactic explanations on a point not grasped by the client through the Socratic dialogue.

Key Idea

Keep to the front of your mind whether to engage a client in Socratic dialogue or give brief didactic explanations when teaching REBT concepts. Be flexible and realise that you will probably need to use both in your therapy work.

Chapter 24

Be Repetitive in Teaching REBT Concepts

You might believe that once you have taught an REBT concept (e.g. awfulising) to your clients, checked their comprehension of the concept, it should 'sink in'; then you can move on to teaching the next concept. Even if your clients do explain in their own words their understanding of the concept, it may not have made any impact upon them in terms of thinking, feeling or behaving differently. In this dialogue, the trainee accepts that the client hasn't understood the REBT concept and proceeds to respond accordingly.

Trainee: What demand were you making when you got angry about the queue moving so slowly?

Client: I wanted the queue to move more quickly because I was in a hurry.

Trainee: Do you remember what we discussed last session about the differences between rigid and flexible attitudes?

Client: I'm sorry I have forgotten.

Trainee: That's fine. These are new concepts, and it takes some time to grasp them.

Both begin with what you want. For example, I want the queue to move quickly because I am in a hurry. How they differ is that with a flexible attitude, you acknowledge that you don't have to get what you want…

Client: …While with the rigid attitude, I am demanding that I have to get what I want.

DOI: 10.4324/9781003423348-26

Trainee:	So, when you were angry were you holding a flexible attitude or a rigid attitude?
Client:	Definitely rigid. I was demanding that because I was in a hurry and wanted the queue to move more quickly, then it had to do so.
Trainee:	Do you want to make a note about the difference between a flexible attitude and a rigid one as it's likely that we will return to this issue again?
Client (picking up a pen and already writing):	I'm doing that right now.

Repeating REBT ideas does not have to be a monotonous affair but, instead, can provide you with opportunities to display your creativity (see Dryden 2024).

Key Idea

Repeat REBT principles until they become part of your clients' healthy, flexible and non-extreme outlooks.

Chapter 25

Explain the Purpose of an Intervention Before Making It

Explaining the purpose of an intervention before you proceed with it is good practice in REBT since doing so treats the client as an active participant in the therapeutic process.

Here is how a therapist explains the purpose of examining the client's attitudes before doing so.

Therapist:	So, what we have done so far is to identify the adversity at the heart of your problem, your disturbed responses to this adversity, what would constitute healthy responses to this adversity, and both the rigid and extreme attitudes that underpin the problem and the alternative flexible and non-extreme attitudes that underpin your healthy response. Is that right?
Client:	That's correct.
Therapist:	So, what I want to do now is to ask you some questions about both sets of attitudes to help you to decide which set you want to go forward with and which set you wish to relinquish. Is that OK with you?
Client:	That's fine.
Therapist:	Do you have any questions before I begin?
Client:	No, everything is clear.

DOI: 10.4324/9781003423348-27

Key Idea

Before an intervention, explain the purpose of it to your clients so that they understand what you are about to do.

Part 2

Good Assessment Practice in REBT

Chapter 26

Help Your Clients to Be Specific When They Are Vague in Describing Their Problems

Specificity is a guiding principle in REBT so that you will want clear and precise information from your clients regarding the *ABC* of their presenting problems. Some clients will communicate in an imprecise, vague way that appears to describe the problem but actually says nothing much at all. If this happens, then you may need to work patiently to help the person be clear. In the following example, note how the therapist steadily helps the client to become more specific about their problem.

Client:	It's something to do with relationships.
Therapist:	'Something to do with relationships' doesn't help us to define what the problem is. Let me see if I can help you be more specific. Is that OK?
Client:	Yes, please.
Therapist:	Fine. With respect to relationships, is the problem with forming them, maintaining them or their end?
Client:	I think the problem concerns maintaining relationships.
Therapist:	What prevents you from maintaining them?
Client:	It's that whole intimacy thing, you know what I mean?
Therapist:	What is it with respect to intimacy that you are troubled about?
Client:	Expressing that other side of myself to others.
Therapist:	Do you mean showing your feelings to others, your sensitive side?
Client:	Yes.

DOI: 10.4324/9781003423348-29

Therapist: And if you show your sensitive side to others?

Client: They may take advantage of it, exploit me, something like that.

Therapist: How would you feel if that happened?

Client: I would feel very hurt. So it's easier to avoid relationships.

Therapist: So you are afraid of intimacy in relationships in case others take advantage and exploit you in some way and you would feel hurt if that happened. Is that right?

Client: Yes.

Therapist: Can we take an example of a relationship which you would like to be more intimate in but are afraid to do so?

Key Idea

Work patiently to help your clients to be more specific when they are vague about their problems.

Chapter 27

When Clients Want to Talk at Length about Their Feelings, Explain REBT's Attitude-Based Model of Change

REBT seeks to discover and examine the rigid and extreme attitudes that underpin clients' disturbed feelings, not focus excessively on the disturbed feelings themselves. Ellis (1991: 6) suggests that 'many clients, some of them trained to do so by previous therapy, long-windedly and compulsively talk about their feelings, their feelings, their feelings'. You might believe that indulging your clients in endless 'feeling talk' will ameliorate their emotional problems. However, REBT is an attitude-based theory of emotional disorders: emotional amelioration occurs through quickly identifying, examining and changing disturbance-inducing attitudes. Ironically, venting disturbed feelings is a highly cognitive activity in which rigid and extreme attitudes that give rise to these disturbed emotional reactions are rehearsed. Giving vent to feelings thus serves to further strengthen the attitudes that account for the disturbance so that, in effect, 'the client actually practices being disturbed. As a result, s/he gets worse rather than better' (Grieger and Boyd 1980: 118).

When a client seems intent on talking at length about their disturbed feelings, the therapist needs to intervene and explain REBT's perspective.

Therapist:	May I interrupt you?
Client:	Sure.
Therapist:	Do you find talking about your problem-related feelings helpful?
Client:	Yes, I do.
Therapist:	Can I give you REBT's perspective on this issue?
Client:	Please.

DOI: 10.4324/9781003423348-30

Therapist: Identifying your disturbed feelings is important because it helps us to discover and examine the rigid and extreme attitudes that underpin these feelings. There is a danger that the more you talk about such feelings, the more you rehearse and entrench these attitudes so that while you may feel better, you may not get better. So instead, we need to acknowledge your disturbed feelings but use them to help you to change the attitudes that are responsible for them.

If the client accepts the therapist's rationale, then they can proceed to an *ABC* assessment of the client's nominated problem. If not, the therapist may need to effect a suitable referral to a therapist who practises in a way that is consistent with what the client wants.

Key Idea

Help your clients to see that emotional change is derived from attitude change, not from excessive discussion of their disturbed feelings.

Chapter 28

Ask for a Specific Example of Your Clients' Nominated Problem

As mentioned earlier, in this book I refer to the problem that a client has elected to discuss with the therapist in the session as the 'client's nominated problem'. Once this problem has been agreed as the session's focus, it is best understood through specific examples of its occurrence – these examples put flesh on the bones of the nominated problem. These specific examples are more likely to provide you with accurate information about your clients' thoughts, feelings and behaviours than a general or abstract discussion of the problem. Your clients' level of emotional engagement with the problem is usually higher at the specific level than the general level. Having said this it is good practice to work with one specific example of the nominated example at a time. This may be:

- A typical example
- A recent example
- A vivid or memorable example
- An anticipated example

Working with an anticipated example is particularly useful when the client's level of avoidance means that they cannot recollect an example of the problem because they do not have one. This often happens with anxiety, in particular. The client says that they are anxious about public speaking, but they have avoided all opportunities to speak in public. Asking them to imagine doing so in the future will provide the level of specificity needed to carry out an REBT-based assessment of the problem.

DOI: 10.4324/9781003423348-31

Client: I am anxious about talking to women that I am attracted to.

Therapist: Can you give me a specific example of this problem.

Client: No, because I don't talk to women that I am attracted to.

Therapist: I understand, but it sounds like you want to talk to them and you would if you weren't anxious. Is that right?

Client: Yes.

Therapist: Is there a woman you are attracted to at the moment?

Client: Yes, a woman in my social group.

Therapist: When is the next time you will be seeing her?

Client: Over the weekend in the wine bar.

Therapist: If you weren't anxious what would you say to her?

Client: I would ask her how her week has gone and what plans she has for the following week?

Therapist: What would you be anxious about that would lead you not to do so.

Client: She would see that I am going red. I go red if I fancy someone.

Therapist: What is anxiety-provoking for you about her seeing you going red?

[Here the therapist has taken a general statement of the clients nominated problem and helped the client create a specific anticipated example of the problem to assess.]

If you find it difficult to locate or work with a specific example of your client's nominated problem, you might find the following points helpful. A specific example occurs at a specific time in a specific place and with specific people present (if relevant). By making the example as concrete as possible, a video- or audio-recording could be made of it (imagine trying to make a recording of a general example).

Key Idea

Make it a habit to ask your clients for a specific example of their nominated problem. Help the client to make the details of this example as clear as possible.

Chapter 29

Check that a Rigid/ Extreme Attitude Is Your Clients' Problem

It is important that you pay attention to understanding your clients' problems from their viewpoint. They may not think that they have an emotional problem and, indeed, may not actually have one. Thus, their problem may be alleviated not by developing flexible and non-extreme attitudes but by developing important skills such as social and study skills. Furthermore, at times the solution to their problem may be to leave an abusive situation (at home or at work) and they need support from you to do this.

Even when a client may have an emotional problem, it is important to understand how they see what determines it. Not all clients will accept that their emotional problems are determined by rigid/extreme attitudes and, in this circumstance, you need to be flexible enough as a therapist to work creatively with the client's perspective and not impose REBT's viewpoint. So, don't be in a rush to find a rigid attitude and its extreme attitude derivatives as an explanation of your client's problems without working carefully to help them to see that.

Key Idea

Understand your clients' problems from their perspective before putting forward your hypothesis that these problems are underpinned by rigid/extreme attitudes. Sometimes, clients' problems are due to some other variables.

DOI: 10.4324/9781003423348-32

Chapter 30

Help Clients to Make Imprecise Emotional Cs Precise

REBT is primarily focused on emotional problem solving (i.e. disturbed or unhealthy negative emotions, such as depression, guilt, shame, hurt and unhealthy anger). When clients are asked about how they feel in response to adverse life events, they will often reply with such terms as 'stressed out', 'bad' and 'upset'. Which unhealthy negative emotions do these terms refer to? This needs to be clarified before an examination of the emotion begins.

Here is an example:

Client: I'm upset when I miss my deadlines at work.

[The client has used an imprecise term, 'upset', to describe their feelings.]

Trainee: When you say 'upset', I am not clear what emotion that refers to. Can you be more precise?

Client: I get angry.

[The trainee is unsure whether this anger is healthy or unhealthy so they will attempt to clarify this.]

Trainee: Is that angry feeling healthy where you are focused on your behaviour but are not attacking yourself or is it unhealthy where you are attacking yourself?

Client: I am attacking myself so it's unhealthy.

A good way to establish the presence of an unhealthy negative emotion is to spell out what you are looking for: 'When you say 'upset',

DOI: 10.4324/9781003423348-33

do you mean unhealthy anger, anxiety shame, for example?' This can begin your client's education about unhealthy negative emotions.

Another vague description of *C* is through the use of inferences.

Trainee:	How do you feel about not being invited to the party?
Client:	I felt rejected by my friends.
Trainee:	Rejection is what you think your friends did to you, it's not a feeling. How do you feel about being rejected?

['Rejected' is an inference, not an emotion. Here the trainee points this out and asks for the feeling again.]

Client:	I felt very hurt.

An important caveat here is that while it is good practice to help clients to be precise about their emotions, it is important not to pressurise them to be any more precise than they can be. Otherwise, you will threaten the working alliance between you and them.

Key Idea

Ensure that you help your clients be precise in labelling their disturbed feelings without pressurising them to do so.

Chapter 31

Explain Why Disturbed Feelings Are Unhealthy/Unhelpful and Why Non-Disturbed Feelings Are Healthy/Helpful

REBT makes the important distinction between unhealthy and healthy negative emotions (e.g. anxiety vs. concern, respectively). While it can be difficult for your clients to see clearly the differences between these emotional states, the distinction between disturbed and non-disturbed *Cs* can serve to give a clear focus to one of the main goals in therapy: 'transforming suffering into appropriate, adaptive, albeit negative emotions' (Walen et al. 1992: 92).

It is particularly tricky to help clients distinguish between healthy and unhealthy anger, but this therapist does it particularly well.

Client: I was really angry when somebody pushed in front of me in the queue. I felt like punching him and was thinking about it throughout the concert.

Therapist: Do you think your anger was healthy or unhealthy?

Client: I thought anger was anger full stop.

Therapist: Can I explain the differences between healthy and unhealthy anger and relate it to the example you just mentioned?

[Note that the therapist first asks for permission to proceed. When the client gives their permission, they are more likely to listen to the therapist than if the latter launched into this distinction without seeking the client's permission.]

Client: Please do.

Therapist: Both types of anger signal to you that the other person behaved badly. Is it healthy to want to punch the person or to assert yourself with them?

DOI: 10.4324/9781003423348-34

Client: I guess assertion is healthier.

Therapist: Is it healthier to ruminate angrily on the person's behaviour so that you can't concentrate on the concert or to let your anger go so that you can concentrate?

Client: Letting it go.

Therapist: So, would you prefer to feel the kind of anger that leads you to want to punch someone and ruminate angrily on what they did or the kind of anger that leads you to assert yourself with the person and to let the incident go?

Client: Definitely, the second. I can see now that the anger I felt wasn't very healthy.

It is useful to emulate what the therapist in the above example did. They contrasted the behaviour or action tendency of both the disturbed emotion and the non-disturbed emotion and the thinking that was associated with both emotions.

When your clients acknowledge that their disturbed emotions are unhealthy, do not assume that their emotional goal is to change them for healthy or non-disturbed feelings. If some clients are reluctant or ambivalent about this proposed emotional shift, undertake a cost-benefit analysis of keeping vs. changing the disturbed feelings.

Key Idea

Take time to help clients see what constitutes unhealthy and healthy negative emotions. Encourage your clients to adopt the latter emotions as their emotional goals.

Chapter 32

Treat Frustration as an *A* Rather than a *C*, But Be Prepared to Be Flexible

Clients often see frustration as a *C*, synonymous with anger. When this is the case, your task as an REBT therapist is to help both of you discover whether such frustration is healthy or unhealthy and proceed from there.

However, REBT theory views frustration as an *A* representing a block or obstacle that a person experiences to their pursuit of a goal. In this case, your task is to discover what the client's feelings were about the frustration and whether these negative feelings were healthy or unhealthy.

In the following excerpt, the supervisor helps the supervisee work more productively with frustration as an *A* rather than a *C*.

Supervisor: You seem to assume that the client's frustration is an unhealthy negative emotion.

Supervisee: He's frustrated about his workload piling up.

Supervisor: His frustration could act as a source of motivation to do something constructive about his workload.

Supervisee: Good point. So how can I find out if his frustration is helpful or not?

Supervisor: One way is to treat his frustration about his workload as an *A*, then ask him whether it is bearable or not.

Supervisee: And if it's unbearable?

Supervisor: Then that probably points to a disturbed emotion like unhealthy anger or anxiety which you can help him with. Or it may point to unhelpful

DOI: 10.4324/9781003423348-35

behaviours such as procrastination or impulsiveness which you can also help him with.

Supervisee: And if it's bearable?

Supervisor: Discuss with him how he can use his frustration to discover if he can have his workload reduced.

Key Idea

Treat your clients' frustration as an *A* and determine whether their *C* is a healthy or unhealthy negative emotion. If you treat their frustration as a *C*, discover whether it is healthy or unhealthy.

Chapter 33

Learn When to Be Specific about an Emotional C and When to Generalise from It

Emotional *Cs* need to be connected to specific situations in order for accurate assessment information to be collected. This helps your clients to see that their disturbed feelings are generated by the rigid and extreme attitudes that they hold towards these situations, not by the situations themselves (further reinforcing emotional responsibility).

When assessing a specific example of the client's nominated problem and particularly when identifying the client's major disturbed emotion at *C*, the client may generalise to other situations in which they experienced the same emotion. When this happens, it is important for the therapist to bring the client back to the selected example of the nominated problem.

On the other hand, once you have helped your client deal with a number of examples of their nominated problem, you might usefully encourage them to stand back and think of other adversities where they experience the same unhealthy negative emotion. If so is there a theme running through these varied adversities that points to a core rigid/extreme attitude (e.g. 'I must have the approval of others. Without it, I'm no good')? In problem assessment, start with understanding your clients' emotional *C* in specific contexts before attempting generalisations about it.

DOI: 10.4324/9781003423348-36

Key Idea

Remember that your therapeutic focus is required at both the special and general levels of assessment, with respect to emotional *Cs*. Begin with the specific level, moving to the general when you and your client are ready to understand their emotional problems in greater breadth and depth.

Chapter 34

Use Your Clients' Behavioural *Cs* to Identify Their Emotional *Cs*

In REBT's *ABC* framework, *C* stands for behavioural consequences as well as emotional consequences. However, REBT is primarily concerned with finding and ameliorating disturbed emotional *Cs* (e.g. depression). Behavioural *Cs* provide useful information about what the emotional *C* might be.

Therapist:	How did you feel when your friend didn't invite you to dinner when she invited others?
Client:	I don't know.
Therapist:	Well, what did you do when you found out?
Client:	I went to my room and cried.
Therapist:	Tears of...?
Client:	Hurt

A particularly difficult behavioural *C* to assess is procrastination. Procrastination is often a behavioural means of protecting individuals from experiencing disturbed feelings if they engaged in the avoided activity. A common mistake among trainees is to focus on the clients' emotions about procrastination (e.g. guilt, anger, shame) as though these were the key emotional *Cs* to examine, when, in fact, the key ones are 'hidden' by the procrastination. In this excerpt, the therapist does not make this mistake.

DOI: 10.4324/9781003423348-37

Therapist: I understand why you are angry with yourself for not getting on with the task, but it is important to find out what prevents you from getting on with it.
Client: I'm not sure what that is.
Therapist: OK, now really imagine that you are about to get down to the task and you begin to experience a feeling that leads you to put it off. Can you imagine that?
Client: Yes.
Therapist: What would that feeling be?
Client: A tense anxiousness.
Therapist: What would you be anxious about?
Client: That my report might not be up to the high standards my boss demands.
Therapist: And if your report fails to live up to those standards?
Client: I'd be seen as the incompetent one in the team, a label that I really don't want to be attached to me.
Therapist: So, does procrastinating help you to avoid that feared outcome?
Client: At that time, yes.
Therapist: So, what do you need to deal with in order to stop procrastinating?
Client: I need to deal productively with being seen to be the incompetent one in the team.
Therapist: Are you ready to do that?
Client: Yes.

If your clients are unable to identify in the session the 'hidden' emotion underpinning their procrastination, ask them to engage in the avoided activity outside of the session in order to uncover it. When counterproductive behavioural *Cs* (e.g. excessive alcohol consumption) are initiated to avoid experiencing disturbed feelings, encourage your clients to stop the counterproductive behaviour (e.g. cease drinking) and tackle constructively the disturbed feelings that are no longer being 'drowned by the alcohol'.

An important point to remember is that counterproductive behavioural *Cs* can exist in their own right: they are neither tied to disturbed feelings nor 'hide' them. When this is the case, they are treated as *C* in an *ABC* episode, and the episode is assessed in the usual way. Behavioural problem-solving demonstrates the flexibility of REBT in action: namely, that you do not need to elicit a disturbed emotion from your client before therapy can proceed.

Key Idea

Use behavioural *Cs* in order to uncover emotional *Cs,* but there will be occasions when behavioural *Cs* exist in their own right and are tackled that way.

Chapter 35

Pinpoint Your Clients' Adversity at *A*

When your clients talk about adverse events in their lives, it is understandable why some of them might provide you with a great amount of detail about these events (e.g. 'I want to get it out of my system'). However, they can overwhelm you with this mass of detail as well as lose themselves within it. When this happens, it is important that you use several of the skills that I have discussed earlier in this book. First, you need to interrupt the client while first explaining the purpose of the interruption – which is to help you both zero in on what the client is most disturbed about in the problem-related example at *A*. Second, you need to help your client to pinpoint the precise nature of the adversity at *A*. I have devised a technique that I have called 'Windy's Magic Question' (WMQ) – see Dryden (2024) – to help you do this.

Here is how a therapist used this technique to help the client identify their adversity at *A*. In this excerpt, the client is anxious about public speaking. The therapist has already identified the client's emotional *C* (anxiety) and the situation in which the *C* was deemed likely to occur.

Step 1: The therapist asked the client to focus on their disturbed *C*. In this case, anxiety.

Step 2: The therapist then asked the client to focus on the situation in which the client thought they would be anxious. In this case, the client said, *'When I am about to give a public presentation to a group of visiting dignitaries'*.

Step 3: The therapist then asked the client: *'Which ingredient could we give you to eliminate or significantly reduce your anxiety?'* In this case the client said, *'My mind would not go blank'*. The therapist took care that the client did not change the situation (i.e., 'I would not give the presentation').

DOI: 10.4324/9781003423348-38

Step 4: In WMQ, the assumption is made that the opposite to the client's response is likely to be the adversity at *A*. In this case, the therapist assumed that the client's *A* was *'My mind going blank'*, but checked with the client. Thus, the therapist asked, *'So when you think about giving the presentation would you be most anxious about your mind going blank?'* If not, the therapist would use the question again until the client confirms what they were most anxious about in the described situation.

Key Idea

Encourage your clients to pinpoint what their adversity was at *A*. Think about using Windy's Magic Question (WMQ) to help you do this.

Chapter 36

Examine Attitudes at *B* Rather Than Question the Validity of Adversities at *A*

When you are assessing a client's example of their nominated problem, and you have identified their adversity at *A*, it is important to regard this as true, temporarily, even if it is grossly distorted. This will enable you to identify the client's basic rigid/extreme attitude at *B*. Trainees new to REBT find it difficult to resist the temptation to question the *A* if it so obviously distorted, but doing so i) prevents the identification of the *B* and ii) creates in the client's mind that adversities at *A* are crucial instead of peripheral to their emotional problems.

Let's consider how two different trainees dealt with the same client *A*.

Excerpt 1

Trainee: So, you are most anxious about your boss laughing at you when you present your report. Is that correct?

Client: Yes.

Trainee: Where is the evidence that he will laugh at you?

Client: I don't have any, but I am still anxious about it.

Trainee: But it's important that you see the world as it is rather than the way you think it is. So let me ask you a different question. How likely is it that your boss will laugh at you when you give them your report?

Client (haltingly): I guess there isn't any.

Trainee: What will happen if you remind yourself of that the next time you are anxious about your boss laughing at you?

DOI: 10.4324/9781003423348-39

Client (unconvinced): I guess it will help

[Here, by questioning the client's A, the trainee is not using REBT theory to guide their work and also is not paying attention and responding to the client's responses that indicate doubt that this line of questioning is helpful.]

Excerpt 2

Trainee: So, you are most anxious about your boss laughing at you when you present your report. Is that correct?

Client: Yes.

Trainee: Let's suppose, for the moment that he does laugh at you, let's see if we can identify the attitude that is largely responsible for your anxiety in this situation.

[Here, by encouraging the client to assume temporarily that A is true, the trainee is using REBT theory to guide their work and orients the client to the attitudinal base of their anxiety.]

There is a place for questioning the validity of the adversity at *A*. This is usually after you have helped the client to examine the client's attitude and helped them to move forward on the basis of their flexible/non-extreme attitude. It is best not to question the adversity at *A* until you have done this attitude-based work.

Key Idea

When assessing the clients' examples of their nominated problems, elicit the adversity at *A* and do not question its validity, even if it is obviously distorted.

Chapter 37

Pursue Clinically Significant Inferences at *A* Instead of Theoretical Inferences

Inference chaining is a frequently used technique in REBT to identify the adversity at *A*. I prefer to use Windy's Magic Question (WMQ) because when doing so, it is less likely that you will identify theoretical inferences rather than clinically significant ones. In inference chaining, when the client gives you an inference, you ask 'Let's assume that's true, then what?' questions, designed to help the identification of the inference that triggers the client's rigid/extreme attitude. This inference is what I call the adversity at *A* and is the most clinically significant of the inferences in the chain. However, in unskilled hands, where the trainee keeps asking the 'Let's assume that's true, then what?' question, it happens that when the chain ends, your clients are imagining themselves destitute (the novelist, Martin Amis, calls this fear of losing everything 'tramp dread').

When this line of questioning is used by rote without due reflection, the client is providing the therapist with theoretical inferences (i.e. grim events that could occur, but the client is not worried about them) instead of clinically significant inferences (i.e. what the client is actually worried about).

In the following excerpt, the therapist notes when the dialogue is staying into the realm of the theoretical and intervenes to keep the focus on the clinically significant. dialogue.

Therapist:	What would you be anxious about if you are not successful in your new career as a consultant?
Client (visibly tensing):	I'm staking everything on being successful.
Therapist:	If you are not successful, then what?

DOI: 10.4324/9781003423348-40

Client (without affect): I won't get the work?

Therapist: And if you don't get the work?

Client (long pause, very flat and unengaged): I won't be able to pay my mortgage.

[When the client poses a question such as the above that is one indication that they are straying into the realm of the theoretical. Long pauses and lack of affect are also signs that this is happening. All three occur above.]

When you are teasing out an inference chain, it is important to pay attention to verbal, paraverbal, behavioural and affective clues, which indicate you are on the right road to the adversity at *A*. In the above dialogue, the client was visibly tensing at one point, but a few moments later he is displaying no affect. The therapist takes note of this.

Therapist: I think I'm on the wrong track. Let's take a step back. You said, 'I'm staking everything on being successful'. What do you mean by that?

Client (becoming agitated): If I don't make it in my new career, then I will have been deceiving myself about having good judgement in making this career move.

Therapist: And if your judgement turns out to be flawed?

Client (eyes moistening, voice dropping): Then I have let down my family.

Therapist: Is that what you are most anxious about: that if you are unsuccessful in your new career, that you will have let down your family?

Client: Yes, that is what I fear the most.

[The client's actual fear has been uncovered. Notice the difference between the client's present emotional state and how he was when theoretical inferences were being discussed.]

Key Idea

Pay careful attention to the clues offered by your clients that indicate you might be eliciting theoretical inferences instead of clinically significant ones. This is particularly the case when you are using inference chaining.

Chapter 38

Realise that Your Clients' Target Emotions Have Changed

When conducting inference chaining, it is important to keep your client's target emotion as the driving force behind the clinical enquiry (e.g. 'What is anger-provoking in your mind…?') in order to locate the adversity at *A*. However, your client will not always give you inferences associated with the 'driving force' emotion, but ones that suggest the target emotion has changed.

To help you here, it is important that you learn the themes tied to particular emotions (see Dryden 2022a) in order to detect emotional shifts during inference chaining. Also, a change in your clients' target emotion is more likely to occur when the initial target emotion is anxiety. Anxiety involves future-orientated thinking; so when you encourage your clients to bring the future into the present (i.e. assume that the future feared event has occurred), the target emotion often changes.

Therapist: What would you be anxious about if you couldn't answer the questions?

Client: I'd be exposed in the group as an idiot. I'd be an object of derision in the group.

Therapist: Assuming that happened, how would you feel at that point?

Client: I'd feel ashamed.

[The client's feeling has changed from anxiety to shame because in the exploration the predicted adversity has happened.]

Therapist: Ashamed of…?

Client: Being seen as an idiot.

DOI: 10.4324/9781003423348-41

Therapist: And would you agree with the group's judgement of you as an idiot?

Client (avoiding eye contact): Yes, I would.

[It is the client's self-evaluation that leads to shame.]

At this point, you can ask your client whether they want to conduct an *ABC* analysis of future exposure as an 'idiot' associated with their anxiety or one focused on being exposed as an 'idiot' connected with their shame.

Key Idea

Learn the themes associated with particular emotions in order to assist you in detecting emotional shifts, especially during inference chaining. Such shifts are especially likely to occur when the client's target emotion is anxiety.

Chapter 39

When Doing Inference Chaining, Notice When Your Clients Have Provided You with a C Instead of an Inference and Respond Accordingly

During inference chaining, your clients might provide you with behavioural or emotional *Cs* in reply to your questions. When this occurs, it is important to ask 'Why' questions to maintain the search for the client's adversity at *A* (Moore 1988). Compare the two following excerpts. In the first, the trainee treats a *C* as an inference, while in the second, the trainee treats it as a *C* and enquires more about it.

Excerpt 1

Trainee: What did you feel hurt about when your partner turned up an hour late?

Client: That he takes me for granted.

Trainee: And if he does take you for granted, then what?

Client: I could smash his face in.

[This response is a C rather than an inference, but the trainee responds to it as an inference and puts it back in the chain as an inference.]

Therapist: And if you did smash his face in?

Client (matter-of-factly): He would end up in hospital and I would be charged by the police with assault.

[By responding to the C ('I could smash his face in') as an A, the therapist takes a wrong turning and effectively abandons the search for the client's hurt-related adversity. The affect has gone from the client's responses which, as mentioned in Chapter 37, indicates that the pair are dealing with a theoretical inference and not a clinically significant one.]

DOI: 10.4324/9781003423348-42

Excerpt 2

Trainee: What did you feel hurt about when your partner turned up an hour late?
Client: That he takes me for granted.
Trainee: And if he does take you for granted, then what?
Client: I could smash his face in
Trainee: Why do you want to smash his face in?

[This response is a C rather than an inference, and the trainee treats it as a C and asks for a reason why the client felt that way.]

Client: Because he knows I love him, and he doesn't return it
Therapist: And if he doesn't return your love
Client: That I care a lot more for him than he cares for me and that's what hurts the most.

Key Idea

Ask 'why' questions when your clients provide you with *Cs* during inference chaining. Don't treat them as inferences.

Chapter 40

Clarify the 'It'

When clients use the word 'it' (e.g. 'I can't stand it' or 'It makes me angry'), it is not always clear what the 'it' refers to. When this is the case, you will need to clarify the 'it'. As the therapist does in the following excerpt.

Therapist:	What is anger-provoking in your mind about being turned down when you asked Mary for a date?
Client:	Nobody wants to get turned down, do they?
Therapist:	Probably not, but as you were turned down…?
Client:	I can't bear it.
Therapist:	What does the 'it' stand for here?
Client:	Not having a girlfriend when all of my friends do.
Therapist:	So, if none of your friends had a girlfriend, would being turned down by Mary have been unbearable?
Client:	That's a good point. No, that would not have been unbearable. It's not having a girlfriend when they all do that made being turned down by Mary so difficult.

[Careful exploration of what 'it' represented for this client bore fruit in this case.]

DOI: 10.4324/9781003423348-43

Key Idea

Do not take the 'it' for granted. If you are unclear what the client means by 'it', clarify 'it' until you are both clear.

Chapter 41

Use Theory-Driven Questions in Assessing Rigid and Extreme Attitudes and Their Flexible and Non-Extreme Attitude Alternatives

Once you have accurately identified the client's *A* and *C* in the chosen example of their nominated problem, you are ready to move on to identifying their rigid/extreme basic attitudes and their flexible and non-extreme attitude alternatives at *B*. In this chapter, I will cover the most efficient way I have found of accomplishing this difficult task.

Some REBT therapists and trainers recommend asking clients open-ended questions to identify their rigid/extreme attitudes, arguing that to use theory-driven questioning is to put words into clients' mouths. I disagree with this viewpoint. Remember that you will have probably already introduced REBT's *ABC* framework to your client before you have reached this stage (see Chapter 22). If not, now is a really good time to do so. Whenever you have chosen to teach your client the *ABC* framework, use it in the service of identifying both sets of attitudes at *B*.

Given this, why ask your client an open-ended question such as:

- 'What were you telling yourself about *A* to create *C*?'
- 'When you felt *C* about *A,* what was going through your mind?'
- 'What did you think about *A* that led you to feel *C*?'

I say this because, in all probability, when you ask such questions, it is unlikely that your clients will give you their rigid and extreme attitudes. Rather, that will give further inferences and other forms of thinking that do not reflect their attitudes.

In response to the accusation that when you use theory-driven questions to identify the client's basic attitudes at *B* you are putting words into their mouths, I suggest that you give them choices. Here are some examples:

DOI: 10.4324/9781003423348-44

- 'When you felt *C* about *A*, was the attitude that you held "I don't want *A* to occur and therefore it must not" or "I don't want *A* to occur but that does not mean that my desire has to be met"?'
- 'When *A* happened and you felt *C*, was your *C* based on the attitude, "It's awful that *A* occurred" or "It's bad that *A* occurred, but not awful"?'
- 'When you failed at the task at *A*, was your feeling at *C* based on the attitude, "It is bad that I failed, and it proves I am a failure" or "It is bad that I failed but I am not a failure. I am a fallible human being who has failed"?'

Once the client has indicated that their attitude was rigid and extreme, you can ask them how they would feel about *A* if they really believed the flexible or non-extreme alternative attitude. In doing so you are helping them to make both of the *B-C* connections[1] and proposing the healthy response at *C* as a potential goal to aim for.

Windy's Review Assessment Procedure (WRAP) (see Dryden, 2024)

This way of assessing attitudes at *B* is a structured, theory-driven approach which I demonstrate below:

Therapist: So, let's review what we know and what we don't know. OK?

Client: OK.

Therapist: At this point, we know what your emotion is at *C* ('anxiety') and we know what your adversity at *A* is ('your boss may criticise you'). Is that right?

Client: Yes.

Therapist: We also know what your preference is. This is ('I don't want my boss to criticise me').

[The therapist knows this because they are using REBT theory to guide their work. This states that whenever a client has an emotional problem this is based on a preference that they have either for something to happen or for something not to happen (as in the client's case).]

What we don't know yet is which of two attitudes your *C* ('anxiety') is based on – a rigid attitude or a flexible attitude.[2] So is your *C* ('anxiety') based on Attitude #1: 'I don't want my boss to criticise me and therefore the must not do so' or Attitude #2: 'I don't want my boss to criticise me, but it doesn't have to be the way I want'.

Client: Attitude number 1.

[If the client does not see that their C ('anxiety') is based on Attitude #1, the therapist would discuss this with them until they understand this 'rigid attitude – unhealthy negative emotion' connection.]

Therapist: Now, if you had strong conviction in Attitude #2, how would you feel about *A* ('your boss criticising you')?

Client: I would feel better, I wouldn't like it but I would not feel anxious.

Therapist: What word would you use to describe that emotion which is the healthy alternative to anxiety?

Client: Concern.

[If the client does not say 'concern' or some suitable synonym, the therapist would discuss this with them until they understand this 'flexible attitude – healthy negative emotion (HNE)' connection.]

Therapist: You now see clearly that your UNE [unhealthy negative emotions] at *C* ('anxiety') is based on your rigid attitude ('I don't want my boss to criticise me and therefore he must not do so') and that the HNE alternative ('concern') is based on your flexible attitude ('I don't want my boss to criticise me, but it doesn't have to be the way I want'). Does it make sense for you to set the concern as your emotional goal in this situation and see that developing conviction in your flexible attitude ('I don't want my boss to criticise me, but it doesn't have to be the way I want') is the best way of achieving this goal?

Client: Very much so.

[If the client has any doubts, reservations or objections to doing so, the therapist would discuss it with them.]

Therapist: Now can you put into your own words what you are going to take away from this?

Key Idea

Use theory-driven questioning as it is the most efficient way of assessing the presence of rigid and extreme attitudes and their flexible and non-extreme attitude counterparts. In doing so, ensure that you engage clients and that you give them an opportunity to clarify their understanding of the points made.

Notes

1 These are the rigid/extreme attitude (*B*) – disturbed response (*C*) connection and the flexible/non-extreme (*B*) – healthy response (*C*) connection
2 The WRAP technique can also be used to identify extreme attitudes and their non-extreme attitude alternatives. See Table 1 in the Introduction for a list of the shared and distinguishing components of rigid and extreme attitudes and their flexible and non-extreme attitudes.

Chapter 42

Do Not Assume that Your Clients Hold All Four Rigid/Extreme Attitudes

When you are teaching your clients about rigid attitudes and their derivatives as part of your assessment of the disturbance-creating attitudes, it is important not to assume they hold all four attitudes. If you do assume this, you may listen for disconfirming evidence.

REBT theory holds that while rigid attitudes are at the core of emotional disturbance certain forms of disturbance are associated with different extreme attitudes. For example:

- Problems of guilt and shame are underpinned by rigid and self-devaluation attitudes
- Frustration-based unhealthy anger is underpinned by rigid attitudes and attitudes of unbearability
- Non-ego anxiety is underpinned by rigid and awfulising attitudes.

However, when working with a particular client with a particular nominated emotional problem, a good rule of thumb is to identify with them a rigid attitude and the one derivative attitude that they resonate with the most as underpinning their problem.

Therapist:	So, you can see that the reason why you are anxious about being criticised by your boss is that you hold a rigid attitude towards such criticism, 'My boss must not criticise me'. Correct?
Client:	Yes, I can see that.
Therapist:	Help me to understand which one of the following three other attitudes you think underpins your anxiety. OK?

DOI: 10.4324/9781003423348-45

Client: OK

Therapist: The choice is i) It's awful if my boss criticises me; ii) I could not bear it if my boss criticises me and iii) if my boss criticises me it means I am inadequate or some other form of self-devaluation. Which one do you resonate with as underpinning you anxiety?

Client: Definitely, the self-devaluation attitude. But it's more like, I'm stupid rather than I'm inadequate.

Key Idea

Do not assume that your clients hold all four rigid/extreme attitudes. Carefully check this out with them. Help them select the one extreme attitude that they think accounts for their problem along with their rigid attitude.

Chapter 43

Distinguish Between Absolute and Preferential Shoulds

When you are assessing for the presence of a rigid attitude, a client may say, for example, 'I should have got straight A grades in my exams'. They have used what I refer to as the unqualified should (Dryden 2022c). As such, you don't know whether the 'should' is absolute or preferential. REBT theory states that only absolute shoulds are rigid and therefore at the core of clients' emotional problems. Given this uncertainty, it is important that you clarify with the client what type of should to which they refer. Otherwise, your client may think that what is a preferential should is absolute.

My suggestion is that you encourage clients to be specific about their unqualified should. Walen et al. (1992: 116) suggest 'it would be wise for the therapist who hears a "should" to rephrase the sentence and feed it back, to ensure that it represents demandingness'.

Therapist: When you say, 'I should have got straight A grades in my exams', do you mean you *absolutely* should have got them, there is no room in your thinking for accepting that you did not get straight A grades? Or do you mean that ideally you should have got these grades, but that you didn't have to do so.

Client: I mean that I cannot and will not accept the results. I absolutely should have got top marks in all my subjects.

[The meaning of the client's 'should' is now clear. It is rigid.]

DOI: 10.4324/9781003423348-46

For a discussion of the different meanings of the word 'should', see Dryden (2022c).

Key Idea

Ensure that you distinguish between absolute, disturbance-creating shoulds and preferential, non-disturbance-creating shoulds.

Chapter 44

Refrain from Constructing a General Version of Your Clients' Situation-Specific Rigid/Extreme Attitude Unless You Have Evidence to Do So

Your clients can hold rigid attitudes in specific as well as general contexts (e.g. 'I must make you see my viewpoint on this issue' and 'People must understand my viewpoint on all issues that I discuss with them' respectively). When you undertake an *ABC* analysis of a specific example of your client's target problem, you are more likely to elicit a situation-specific rigid/extreme attitude than a general one. Unless you have evidence that the client holds a general version of a rigid/extreme attitude do not assume that they do. Check it out.

Therapist: So, we have established that you are anxious about being criticised by your boss because your attitude towards this is, 'I must not be criticised by my boss and I am stupid if this happens'. Is that right?

Client: Yes.

Therapist: Can I just check something with you. Do you hold this attitude generally or is it only with your boss?

Client: It's not with everyone, but it's when I see that others have some control over what I want.

Key Idea

When you elicit a situation-specific rigid/extreme attitude, work on that attitude until, and only until, further evidence is uncovered that the attitude is a specific example of a more general problem. Check this out with your clients before moving to the general level.

DOI: 10.4324/9781003423348-47

Chapter 45

Express Self-Devaluation in Your Clients' Words

People often devalue themselves when their rigid demands are not met (e.g. the depression-inducing attitude, as in: 'I didn't get the job, which I absolutely should have done, this means I'm a failure'). When people think in this way, it is called 'ego disturbance'. Sometimes it can appear in REBT that ego disturbance is defined scatologically: 'self-esteem…depends on your doing the right thing, and when you do the wrong thing, back to shithood you go…shouldhood equals shithood' (Albert Ellis, quoted in Bernard 1986: 52–3). You might believe that self-devaluation is simply clients calling themselves 'shits'. clients' self-devaluing epithets (e.g. worthless, useless) are not necessarily synonymous in their minds with 'shithood' and, therefore, you need to be very wary about introducing the term as a matter of course. In fact, introduce it only when your clients actually call themselves 'shits'. Much better to use your clients' form of self-devaluation as this will keep you alert to the manifold ways ego disturbance is expressed.

Client: That self-help book you lent me upset me because it says people call themselves 'shits' when things go wrong. I don't call myself that. I was quite offended.

Therapist: I think the book was making a general point. It is much better and more accurate to locate the precise words people use when they put themselves down. What would you call yourself for starting drinking again?

DOI: 10.4324/9781003423348-48

[The therapist does not get sidetracked by the client's A-C thinking – what he read in the book upset him – and focuses on eliciting his idiosyncratic expression of self-devaluation.]

Client: I'm a fraud. I promised myself and others that I would never drink again.

Key Idea

Let your clients describe self-devaluation in their own ways. Do not force any particular language (e.g. 'shithood') on them.

Chapter 46

Clearly Determine Whether Ego or Discomfort Disturbance Is the Primary Problem

REBT posits two types of emotional disturbance underlying most, if not all, neurotic problems: ego and discomfort. Ego disturbance involves self-devaluation, while discomfort disturbance views prevailing life conditions as unbearable. While ego and discomfort disturbance are seen as discrete categories, they frequently interact. Therefore, you are advised to be alert to problems in both these areas and, when they interact, careful assessment is required to disentangle one from the other. Often, trainees will too readily assume, for example, that avoidance of an onerous task involves discomfort disturbance, while it may involve ego disturbance or both. In the following excerpt, it turns out that ego disturbance is the main issue for the client although at first sight it appears to be discomfort disturbance.

Client:	It's going to be a major hassle getting on with the essay when it's party season.
Therapist:	What's stopping you from getting on with it?
Client:	I can't bear the thought of all that research I've got to do.
Therapist:	Your attitude to the work reflects what is known in REBT as 'discomfort intolerance'. It sometimes is also referred to as an attitude of unbearability.
Client (smiles):	That sure sounds like me.

While 'procrastination almost always involves discomfort intolerance' (Wessler and Wessler 1980: 104), it does not mean that this is

DOI: 10.4324/9781003423348-49

always the primary disturbance underpinning procrastination, as the therapist discovers in the excerpt below.

Therapist: If I was able to help you face the 'major hassle' of the research for the essay, would you then be able to get on with it?

Client: If I started on the essay, that would bring up another worry: I might not get a high mark.

Therapist: What would that mean to you, if you didn't get a high mark?

Client: I'd be a failure, big time.

Therapist: So which problem is the greater obstacle for starting the essay: discomfort intolerance or seeing yourself as a failure when you don't get a high mark?

Client: The failure part. I get a tight stomach just thinking about it.

[Ego disturbance is the primary problem: 'I must get a high mark and if I don't, I'd be a failure'.]

On the other hand, what seems an obvious case of ego disturbance may not be:

Therapist: What are you anxious about with regard to that talk in a few weeks' time?

Client: Who wants to make a fool of themselves? I'm sure there'll be some questions I can't answer and gaps in my knowledge will be exposed. I'll have to do a lot of preparatory reading to try and avoid that happening. I might actually cancel the talk.

Therapist: So, if these things occur, you'll see yourself as a fool and that's why you're thinking about cancelling the talk. Is that right?

Client: Yes, that's right.

At first blush, it seems like a case of ego anxiety about making a fool of themself, but the client did refer to having to do a lot of 'preparatory reading' for the talk.

Therapist: Won't the preparatory reading increase the probability of answering all the questions and plugging gaps in your knowledge and thereby reducing the chances of you looking like a fool?

Client: Probably, but reducing the chances of looking like a fool means a hell of a lot of work in the next few weeks, a hell of a lot. It will do my head in.

Therapist: Can I just clarify something with you: what are you most anxious about – the preparatory reading or looking like a fool?

Client: All that preparatory stuff. I really cannot be bothered to do it.

Therapist: And is that the real reason you're thinking about cancelling the talk?

Client: Yes, it is.

[Discomfort disturbance is the primary problem: 'I absolutely shouldn't have to work this hard to be knowledgeable for the talk. It's too hard, and I can't bear it!']

When ego and discomfort aspects of the problem appear equally strong, discuss with your client which aspect to work on first. With regard to assessing emotional disturbance, it is important to remember that rigid attitudes on their own do not give a clue as to whether your client's problem is basically ego or discomfort in nature. Rigid attitudes plus self-devaluation attitudes (especially when these latter attitudes are stronger than any attitudes of unbearability present) point to ego disturbance, while rigid attitudes plus attitudes of unbearability (with the presence of only weak self-devaluation attitudes) suggest discomfort disturbance. Rigid attitudes plus awfulising attitudes offer no reliable guide to pinpointing a client's problems as mainly ego or discomfort related. Assess the awfulising attitude to determine this. For example, a client says that the end of his marriage is awful: does this refer to seeing himself as a failure or living alone will be unbearable?

If the client focuses on seeing themself as a 'failure', this indicates that awfulising is mainly associated with ego disturbance.

Key Idea

Go beyond prima facie evidence of your clients' ego or discomfort disturbance to assess carefully whether your initial impressions are correct.

Chapter 47

Look for a Meta-Emotional Problem

One of the unique features of REBT is its emphasis on meta-emotional disturbances, or what some other REBT therapists refer to as secondary emotional disturbances (Ellis and Bernard 1985), in other words, our ability to disturb ourselves about our primary emotional disturbances, e.g. unhealthy anger about feeling anxious or being ashamed of feeling unhealthily jealous. The presence of a meta-emotional problem can hinder your client's progress in therapy on their primary nominated problem, e.g. you are tackling your client's unhealthy jealousy, while he is unhealthily angry with himself for feeling jealous. Unless there is an agreed focus on the primary or meta-emotional problem, the therapist and client will jump from one to another and back again, engendering client and therapist confusion. The therapist in the excerpt identifies the client's meta-emotional problem and agrees a focus for their subsequent work.

Therapist: Can you provide a specific example of your angry outburst towards your wife?

Client: You know, I really shouldn't behave like this. It's unacceptable to be angry with people you care for and who care for you.

[The client is signalling the possible presence of another emotion, which seems to be distracting him from responding to the therapist's questions.]

Therapist: I get the impression that you are distracted in some way, and therefore you are not focused on my question. Would my assumption be correct?

DOI: 10.4324/9781003423348-50

(client nods) Is it to do with your unacceptable behaviour? *(client nods)* How do you feel when you think about yourself in this way and the way you've treated your wife?

Client: I feel so guilty. I promise to change my ways, but I don't.

[At this point, the therapist and client can decide whether guilt should now replace unhealthy anger as the focus of clinical attention.]

You can routinely enquire about a meta-emotional problem as soon as your clients reveal a primary emotional problem, wait until the primary problem has been assessed first or probe for it only when your clients are not making the expected progress on their primary problem.

Key Idea

Be alert for the possible presence of meta-emotional problems.

Chapter 48

Do Not Assume that a Meta-Emotional Problem Is Always Present

Determining whether or not a meta-emotional problem is present is part of the REBT assessment process. However, determining (e.g. 'I wonder if there is one?') does not mean predetermining (i.e. 'It'll be there'). The REBT literature does say that clients frequently disturb themselves about their emotional problems, but it is important that you do not convert 'frequently' into 'always'.

Even if a client does have a meta-emotional problem, it does not follow that they will want to deal with it. Many years ago, an REBT colleague, Dr. Al Raitt, established a weight control clinic in Bristol in the West of England. I remember him telling me that most of his clients had meta-emotional problems concerning their difficulties with losing weight. However, very few of them wanted to target this secondary problem for change. Al told me his clients told him, 'I'm here for weight loss. I haven't come for psychotherapy'.

Key Idea

Remember that meta-emotional problems may be present but not always so. Be open-minded in looking for their presence.

DOI: 10.4324/9781003423348-51

Chapter 49

Decide with Clients Whether or Not to Work on Their Meta-Emotional Problem First

If you have detected a meta-emotional problem, it does not automatically follow that you should start working on it there and then. I suggest using four criteria for working on your client's meta-emotional problem before their primary emotional problem:

1. When the meta-emotional problem interferes with your work on the primary problem.
2. When the presence of the meta-emotional problem interferes with your client's between-sessions task on their primary problem.
3. When the meta-emotional problem is clinically more important than the primary problem.
4. When your client sees the sense of tackling their meta-emotional problem before their primary problem.

Perhaps the final criterion is the most important since that without the client's agreement, working unilaterally on the meta-emotional problem would threaten the working alliance.

Therapist: So, when you stand back and think about being anxious about your boss's criticism, how do you feel about making yourself anxious about this.

Client: I feel really angry with myself. I really should not let him get to me.

Therapist: Will your anger at yourself interfere with the work we need to do on your anxiety problem in sessions?

Client: I don't think so.

DOI: 10.4324/9781003423348-52

Therapist: And will this interfere with the work you'll need to do between sessions?
Client: No.
Therapist: Which problem shall we focus on?
Client: Definitely my anxiety problem.

Key Idea

Only work on the meta-emotional problem first if one or more of the four criteria are met.

Part 3

Good Goal-Setting Practice

Chapter 50

Distinguish Between the Two Stages of Goal-Setting

There are usually two goal-setting stages in the initial assessment of your client's presenting problem:

1. When your client states the problem and goal in general terms (the 'problem as defined').
2. After the problem has been explored in *ABC* terms and the problem and goal have now been made specific (the 'problem as assessed').

It is important to cover both stages.

Stage 1: Goal related to the problem as defined

Therapist:	What problem would you like to start with in therapy?
Client:	I am anxious about talking to people that I don't know.
Therapist:	What would you like to achieve from therapy on this problem?
Client:	I would like to speak to people I don't knowwithout anxiety.

[Here the client has set a goal based on the problem as defined.]

DOI: 10.4324/9781003423348-54

Stage 2: Goal related to the problem as assessed

Therapist:	So, let's recap on our assessment. You are anxious that if you talk to someone you don't know they will think you are stupid at *A* and that would prove you are stupid at *B*. Instead of being anxious about strangers thinking you are stupid, what would be your emotional goal?
Client:	Well, I wouldn't like it, but I don't want it to stop me from talking to people.
Therapist:	What would you call that feeling?
Client:	You mentioned non-anxious concern earlier. That would work for me.

[Here the client has set a goal based on the problem as assessed.]

Key Idea

Goal-setting occurs when your client's problem is defined and after it has been assessed.

Chapter 51

Achieve a Balance Between Your Clients' Short- and Long-Term Goals

REBT argues that we are likely to be at our happiest when enjoying the pleasures of the moment and planning constructively for the future (known as long-range hedonism). Clients often pursue short-term goals (e.g. avoidance), which sabotage their long-term goals (e.g. overcoming their anxiety). However, if they are encouraged to forego all forms of short-term pleasure then they will often rebel against what they see as an austere, 'let's think about the long-term' regime.

Therapist: You're falling behind with your studies because you go to too many parties. Is that right?
Client: Yes
Therapist: What is your idea of a good way ahead with respect to falling behind with your studies?
Client: Well, I want to catch up on the work that I have fallen behind on, but I want to have some fun.
Therapist: Can I suggest something as a discussion opener?
Client: Sure.
Therapist: What about studying during the week and partying only at the weekend?
Client: I can live with that.
Therapist: So, let's look at developing an attitude that will help you to study during the week and party at weekends.

DOI: 10.4324/9781003423348-55

Key Idea

Help your clients to reach a balance between pursuing both short- and long-term goals.

Chapter 52

Negotiate Goals that Help to Strengthen Your Clients' Flexible and Non-Extreme Attitudes

Self-helping goals in REBT are those that involve healthy negative emotions and productive behaviours underpinned by flexible and non-extreme attitudes. As such, it is important that you avoid setting goals that unwittingly perpetuate their rigid and extreme attitudes.

Client:	My boyfriend dumped me. I'm nothing without him and I can't live without him. I'll do anything to get him to take me back. I'll beg if I have to.
Therapist:	Is that the goal you would like us to work on: to get him to take you back?
Client:	That's what I want most of all.
Therapist:	If I go along with your goal, then all I'm doing is agreeing with you that you can't live without him, you're nothing without him, and it's all right to grovel before him, begging to be taken back. I wouldn't be helping you to overcome your emotional problems, I'd be helping you to make them worse. What if he doesn't take you back?
Client:	I don't want to think about that.
Therapist:	OK, think about this then: just imagine that you could live without him and be reasonably happy, and stopped believing you are nothing without him, how would you then feel?
Client:	Well, I suppose I'd be much less upset.
Therapist:	And, if you still wanted to get back with him, would you beg?
Client:	No. I would ask, but I wouldn't beg.

DOI: 10.4324/9781003423348-56

Therapist: What would be the difference?

Client: If I asked, that would mean I have self-respect and could live without him, but begging means no self-respect and continuing to be his slave or throwing myself in the river, if he says 'No'.

Therapist: So would you like to work towards a goal where you asked your boyfriend to go back with you but not begged him to do so?

['Asked' is conceptualised by the therapist as being based on healthy negative emotions and flexible/non-extreme attitudes which he will presently discuss with the client.]

Client: Yes, I would like to do that.

[The client is now receptive to seeing constructive ways of dealing with her emotional disturbance.]

Key Idea

Negotiate goals with clients that strengthen their flexible and non-extreme attitudes rather than ones that perpetuate their rigid and extreme attitudes.

Chapter 53

Agree Goals with Clients that Are Within Their Control

Sometimes, clients set goals that are out of their control (e.g. 'I want my boss to stop criticising me'). Such goals are often a reflection of the person's sense of powerlessness or victim status. It is important to teach such clients what is within their power to change or control and what is not; this teaching is missing in this dialogue:

Client: Now that I'm self-employed, I've got to get some work. I haven't got too much money left to pay the bills. I wish some of these companies would give me some work. I'm really angry with the time it's taking.

Therapist: So, your goal is to get some work from some of these companies?

Client: That's right. They need to give me some work and if they do, I'll feel a whole lot better.

[You might think that 'getting some work' is a perfectly reasonable goal, but the therapist discusses the problem with it.]

Therapist: Who actually gives you the work: you or someone in the company you're targeting for the work?

Client: Well, someone in the company.

Therapist: Is that within your control or theirs?

Client: Theirs.

Therapist: What is within your control?

Client: To keep pushing myself forward, not giving up, learning from people who have been self-employed longer than me, that sort of thing.

DOI: 10.4324/9781003423348-57

Therapist: And do you do those things?

Client: No. I suppose I'm expecting quick results and not prepared for the long haul or taking setbacks very well.

[This reply could indicate the client is adhering to an attitude of unbearability.]

Therapist: So, if you learned to be persistent and resilient in facing these difficulties, what then?

[The antidote to an attitude of unbearability is learning and developing an attitude of bearability.]

Client: I suppose I'll be more likely to get work, but no guarantees.

Therapist: So shall we start developing an outlook based on persistence and resilience, something that is within your control?

Client: I do want to succeed in my new career so yes, I would like to do that.

Therapist: Great! Having the right attitude in trying to get the work is just as important as having the talent to do the work when you get it.

With regard to client goals targeted at changing others, it is important to point out that your clients usually have to change first (e.g. become more assertive) before attempting to influence the behaviour of others. Change is within the other person's control, and attempting to influence the other person to change is within your client's control.

Key Idea

Ensure that your clients' goals are within their sphere of control.

Chapter 54

Encourage Your Clients to State Their Goals in Positive Terms

Clients often state their goals as the absence or reduction of a negative state: for example, 'I don't want to feel guilty anymore' or 'I want to feel less anxious'. These goals state how the client does not want to feel or behave (i.e. stated in negative terms), instead of how the client wants to feel or behave (i.e. stated in positive terms).

> Stating goals in positive terms is very important because of the role that goal setting plays in human cognition and performance... When the goal is stated positively, clients are more likely to encode and rehearse the things they want to be able to do rather than the things they want to avoid or stop.
>
> (Cormier and Cormier 1985: 223)

Client: I want to stop feeling anxious and not blush when I'm the centre of attention. Just stop acting like an idiot because people are looking at me.

Therapist: If you want to stop feeling anxious and acting like an 'idiot', how do you want to feel and behave?

Client: I'd like to feel concerned about being the centre of attention and stay in the situation instead of trying to avoid it.

Therapist: And what attitude will accompany this feeling of concern?

Client: That I can accept being the centre of attention without liking it and accept myself for blushing

DOI: 10.4324/9781003423348-58

or acting awkwardly. Do you know what I'd really like to feel in that situation?

Therapist: What's that?

Client: I really want to feel relaxed and confident. Let people look because I'm no longer bothered. That sounds good. I'd really like to achieve those things.

Therapist: OK, that may be possible, and it would probably take two goal-setting stages to achieve. First is to overcome your psychological problem by feeling concerned, not anxious, about being the centre of attention. When you have achieved that, then you can set a personal development goal whereby you feel relaxed and confident when people look at you: you no longer feel concerned when you are the centre of attention.

Client: Good. Let's get working on stage one then.

Key Idea

Ensure that your clients' goals are stated in positive terms, not in negative terms, and are based on flexible and non-extreme attitudes. Sometimes, your clients will have two goals in mind: overcoming their psychological problems and then focusing on some aspect of personal development. Help them to see that the achievement of the first precedes the achievement of the second.

Chapter 55

Focus on Outcome Goals Instead of Process Goals

Some clients come to therapy to immerse themselves in self-exploration (therapeutic process) rather than setting specific goals for change (therapeutic outcome). REBT is problem-focused and outcome-orientated; if you focus on the process, therapy is likely to get bogged down in endless self-analysis and 'feeling talk' (see Chapter 27).

Supervisor: Listening to the session recording, I don't get the impression your client has been introduced to REBT yet.

Supervisee: That's true. He wanted so much to find out why his life is in such a mess, and we've got stuck on it. I don't know how to intervene to set the goals.

Supervisor: To move him from interminable problem describing to problem solving. How do you begin to do that?

Supervisee: Tactfully interrupt him to start with. I suppose I could say to him what goals would he need to pull himself out of the mess, instead of just talking about the mess.

Supervisor: Good. Also, point out to him that working towards those goals not only helps to pull him out of the mess but also helps him to understand how he got into it.

Supervisee: Sounds simple when you say it.

Supervisor: Try it and see what happens. I'll look forward to hearing the results on your next recording.

DOI: 10.4324/9781003423348-59

Key Idea

Focus on outcome goals, not process goals.

Chapter 56

Focus on Emotional Goals Before Practical Goals

REBT advocates that clients face adversities at *A* in an undisturbed manner at *C* before turning to practical problem solving. For example, a person who is angry with a colleague who behaves obnoxiously towards him is encouraged to undisturb himself about the behaviour before deciding on his next step, which might be to learn assertiveness or leave the job – the decision would be made in an undisturbed state. Focusing only on a practical goal, like leaving the job, leaves the emotional disturbance intact (e.g. 'I absolutely shouldn't have to be subject to this behaviour. It's awful') and ready to 'strike' again, if the client meets others who behave in a similar manner towards him.

Client: The relationship is boring. I've been in quite a few of them. 'Get the hell out', that's what I say.

Therapist: Does it ever bother you that you leave a relationship as soon as it gets boring?

Client: Why should I stay?

Therapist: What's the attitude you have to boredom in relationships?

Client: I can't stand it. I like excitement: things happening all the time. I know it sounds childish and I know I'm running away from responsibility, but there it is.

Therapist: Would you like to learn to stay in a so-called boring relationship, put up with these unpleasant feelings until they pass and then decide whether you want to stay or leave? You might even find things

DOI: 10.4324/9781003423348-60

in the relationship to enjoy that you wouldn't be aware of because you're usually long gone.

Client: I wouldn't have to stay after I got over the boredom, would I?

Therapist: You don't have to stay but the point is your choice will be made on the basis of emotional stability, not emotional disturbance. You can prove to yourself that you can tolerate boredom and thereby stop turning a relationship hassle into a relationship horror that you have to immediately leave.

Do not overlook practical goals after the emotional ones have been achieved. Your clients still want to achieve other things in life apart from overcoming their emotional difficulties.

Key Idea

Remember to focus on emotional goals before practical goals.

Chapter 57

Help Your Clients Understand that Intellectual Insight into Flexible and Non-Extreme Attitudes Is Necessary But Not Sufficient for Meaningful Change to Occur

REBT distinguishes between intellectual and emotional insight. The former refers to flexible and non-extreme attitudes lightly and intermittently held and the latter to flexible and non-extreme attitudes deeply and consistently held. Practising a flexible/non-extreme outlook helps clients to move from intellectual to emotional insight. Some clients believe that, if they know why they feel and behave as they do, this would bring a spontaneous improvement in their present functioning without any further effort on their part. In this supervisory dialogue, the supervisor helps the supervisee see that while it is important to have intellectual insight, it is not sufficient for meaningful change to occur.

Supervisor: Listening to the recording, you have done a good job helping your client to develop a set of flexible and non-extreme attitudes to their rigid and extreme attitudes. However, your client seems to think that now they understand what these alternative healthy attitudes are then that understanding will help them achieve their goals.

Supervisee: But such understanding is important, isn't it?

Supervisor: Yes, but your client seems to think that it is sufficient for such change to occur. I couldn't hear you say anything to disabuse them of this idea.

DOI: 10.4324/9781003423348-61

Supervisee: I guess I was so pleased that I was able to help the client recognise alternative flexible and non-extreme attitudes that I was resting on my laurels.

Supervisor: I can understand that but what's the next step with this client?

Supervisee: To help the client see that understanding their flexible and non- extreme attitudes is the first stage of change, not the end stage.

Supervisor: Nice way of putting it. So, your client has intellectual insight into these attitudes, what do they need to do to get emotional insight?

Supervisee: Well, I need to help them see that they now need to keep examining their attitudes and to act forcefully in ways that are consistent with their new flexible and non-extreme attitudes, and if they do this, their conviction in their new attitudes will grow.

Supervisor: I look forward to hearing your next recording with the client where you do that.

[The supervisor has helped the supervisee see that they need to teach their client that intellectual insight plus forceful and persistent daily action brings about therapeutic change. Gaining intellectual insight is the precursor to emotional insight, not the goal of therapy.]

Key Idea

Show your clients why intellectual insight alone is insufficient to bring about personal change; both forms of insight are required.

Chapter 58

Help Your Clients Understand that Feeling Neutral about Negative Events Is Not Healthy

When your clients say they want to feel indifferent or not care about adverse events in their lives, this attitude may appear helpful at first glance. Encouraging clients to feel neutral about adversities at *A* means that they will have to lie to themselves and believe that they don't care about what they do care about. This, of course, is not good therapy. So, if your clients want to feel neutral about adversities dissuade them and explain why. Some trainees go along with this client goal in the mistaken belief that, if you do not care about something, the problem will disappear. In our experience, clients usually do care, and you might be helping them to suppress their healthy desires for bad things not to occur in their lives, as the therapist points out:

Therapist:	You're trying to convince me that you don't give a damn about losing your job. Is that really true?
Client:	If I do give a damn, then I'll be all torn up inside about it. So, it's better to feel nothing.
Therapist:	Isn't the reverse true: you do actually feel something? If I can help you to accept the grim reality of losing your job but without being 'all torn up inside about it', just disappointed for example, would you be prepared to feel something instead of nothing?
Client:	I suppose so. I know that I'm lying to myself about feeling nothing.
Therapist:	And if I help you reinforce that pretence, will that help you in the long-run?
Client:	No, I can see that now.

DOI: 10.4324/9781003423348-62

Key Idea

Help your clients to experience healthy negative emotions about adverse life events rather than to feel neutral about them.

Chapter 59

Help Your Clients Understand that Improved Problem Management Can Be Attained Rather than Cure

A cure may be the ideal of therapeutic intervention, but improvement is the usual reality. Improvement can be measured along the following three dimensions:

1. Frequency – does the problem occur less frequently than before?
2. Intensity – is the problem less severe or intense than before?
3. Duration – does the problem last for shorter periods than before?

Client: I've had such problems with my sleep over the years. It's been so draining, so exhausting. I can't tell you what I've been through. I would love to have an uninterrupted eight hours' sleep every night for the rest of my life. Wouldn't that be wonderful?

Therapist: That would indeed be wonderful. However, can we aim for something that is more realistic and then see what happens?

Client: What would be more realistic?

Therapist: Well, how do you feel about the sleep you are getting now?

Client: Depressed

Therapist: Does depression help you improve your sleep?

Client: No, it does not.

DOI: 10.4324/9781003423348-63

Therapist:	So how about we target that depression first and work towards sleep improvement rather than sleep cure?
Client:	That sounds do-able.

Key Idea

Set goals that are realistic and achievable, using the three dimensions of frequency, intensity and duration.

Chapter 60

Agree Goals with Your Clients that Are Realistic and Ambitious

Your clients' goals should help them to tackle their problems constructively, instead of reinforcing them. For example, a client with perfectionist tendencies may set their goal too high (e.g. to not make any mistakes on my forthcoming projects') thereby making it unachievable, prolonging their procrastination about starting these projects and strengthening their fear of failure. With such clients, it is important to help them set goals that acknowledge their fallibility, deal effectively with setbacks and strive for ambitious standards but not unrealistic ones.

Clients who are unambitious in their goal-setting also usually fear failure and should be shown that their unambitious standards maintain rather than solve their problem. Such clients should be encouraged to be more ambitious in their goal-setting. Challenging goals are more likely to lead to higher performance than 'easy goals' (Cormier and Cormier 1985: 224).

Key Idea

Help your clients to set goals that are neither overwhelmingly high nor underwhelmingly low. Tackle the rigid and extreme attitudes that impel your clients to set such goals.

DOI: 10.4324/9781003423348-64

Chapter 61

Elicit from Your Clients a Commitment to Change

Stating a goal is not the same as being committed to achieving it, e.g. a client states his goal as abstinence from alcohol, but this goal was 'forced' on him by his wife threatening to leave; he wants her to stay and for himself to continue drinking. To be committed to change means undertaking willingly the hard work involved in reaching the goal and seeing clearly the benefits to be gained when the goal is achieved.

If a client is not fully committed to pursuing a goal, it may be important for you to help them evaluate fully the advantages and disadvantages of both the problem state and the alternative goal state. Through a cost-benefit analysis (CBA) of the pros and cons of changing, your client may decide that the goal is more attractive than plodding on with the problem. At this point, you can ask your client for a commitment to the goal. Your client is now more likely to be motivated to change rather than still ambivalent about it.

A therapist used the CBA tool with a client who was ambivalent about addressing his anger. After doing this, the client said:

> I never realized how much grief my anger outbursts caused others or myself until you did that cost-benefit thing; it really brought it home to me. I don't have to be a wimp if I stop being angry; in fact, I'll probably end up a stronger person if I learn to control my temper. I'll certainly give it a go.

DOI: 10.4324/9781003423348-65

Key Idea

Ensure that you elicit from your clients a commitment to change, not just a statement of their goals. If your clients are ambivalent about achieving their goals, carry out a cost-benefit analysis to increase their motivation to change.

Part 4

Good Practice in Examining Attitudes in REBT

Chapter 62

Prepare Your Clients for Examining Their Attitudes

Helping clients to stand back and examine their attitudes[1] (both their rigid and extreme attitudes and their flexible and non-extreme attitudes) is probably one of the most distinctive features of REBT (Dryden 2021a). Examining attitudes can be an uncomfortable or unnerving experience for clients as they are, in essence, being asked to defend their attitudes. In order to pave the way for the attitude examination process and avoid the impression that you are attacking your clients, there are a number of activities to carry out.

First, review the *ABC* of the specific example of your clients' nominated problem; this refreshes their mind about it. Second, ensure that your clients understand the *B-C* connection; this will help them to see the sense in examining *B*. Third, help them to see that their new *C* (goal) is achieved by changing rigid/extreme attitudes at *B* in favour of the alternative flexible/non-extreme attitudes: emotional change flows from attitude change. Fourth, explain to your clients what is involved in the examination process (i.e. an examination of their attitudes) and what is not involved (e.g. arguing, 'brainwashing').

It is important that you temper your enthusiasm to get 'stuck into' helping clients to examine their attitudes and remember the importance of this preparatory stage.

Therapist: So, we have seen that your anxiety of being criticised by your boss is underpinned by the rigid/extreme attitudes that we have up on the whiteboard here and that if you want to be concerned but not anxious about his criticism you need to

DOI: 10.4324/9781003423348-67

develop these alternative flexible and non-extreme attitudes. Is that clear?

Client: Yes, you have helped me to be clear about that.

Therapist: Now, the first step in this attitude change process is seeing which set of attitudes are true, logical and helpful and which are false, illogical and unhelpful. Would you like your attitudes to be true, logical and helpful or false, illogical and unhelpful?

Client: True, logical and helpful, of course.

Therapist: So, if it's OK with you, I will ask you to examine both sets of attitudes to determine their status on the true/false, logical/illogical and helpful/unhelpful criteria. OK?

Client: OK.

Therapist: I will do that by asking you a series of questions and to have you explain the reasons for your answers. Any questions about what we are going to do?

Client: No. I'm ready to go.

Key Idea

Prepare your clients for the process of examining their attitudes. Do not just plunge into it.

Note

1 In this book, when discussing 'examining attitudes' I refer to examining both a client's rigid/extreme attitudes and their flexible/non-extreme attitudes unless it is clear to the contrary.

Chapter 63

Examine Attitudes Creatively, Not Mechanically

There are three major ways of examining attitudes in REBT:

1. *Using empirical arguments.* Is an attitude true or false? Does it correspond with empirical reality or not?
2. *Using logical arguments.* Given that an attitude has two parts (e.g. 'I want to succeed…therefore I have to do so' or 'I want to succeed…but sadly I don't have to do so'), does the second part follow logically from the first?
3. *Using pragmatic arguments.* Does an attitude help the client achieve their goals or hinder them?

Learning to help clients examine their attitudes is like learning jazz. Begin by learning the structure of examining these attitudes and then use this as a platform for improvisation. In my experience, it is the therapists who do this that are the most effective REBT practitioners.

The Choice-Based Examination Method (see Dryden, 2024)

What is the structure of examining attitudes? I developed such a structure which I have called the choice-based examination method. It allows you to bring order to the attitude-examining process in that you focus on one rigid or extreme attitude at a time together with the alternative flexible and non-extreme attitude and ask the same question of each.

As just stated, you can employ the choice-based method with your client's rigid attitude and the flexible alternative to this attitude and/or the most relevant extreme attitude and the non-extreme alternative to this attitude. While using it you basically ask your client to focus on

DOI: 10.4324/9781003423348-68

both attitudes and to choose which is true and which is false, which is logical and which is illogical and which is healthy and which is unhealthy and to give reasons for their choice. This is why I call this examination process 'dialectical' since dialectical means resolving opposing viewpoints through the use of reasoned arguments, which is a good description of the purpose of examining attitudes in REBT.

Using the Choice-Based Examination Method with Rigid and Flexible Attitudes

When using this method[1] with your client's rigid and flexible attitudes, encourage them to focus on both attitudes and ask them the following questions:

- Which of these two attitudes is true or consistent with reality and which is false or inconsistent with reality and why?
- Which of these two attitudes is logical or sensible and which is illogical or nonsensical and why?
- Which of these two attitudes is largely helpful to you and which is largely unhelpful to you and why?
- Which of these attitudes do you want to choose to develop going forward and why?

When the client gives you the 'right' answer, it is important that they are able to provide good reasons that underpin their response. Don't just listen to the content of the arguments. Listen also to the tone in which the arguments are presented, for the tone often belies the client's true viewpoint. If you suspect that they are harbouring a doubt, reservation or objection to a flexible/non-extreme attitude, help them to express this and deal with what emerges.[2]

Developing Creativity in Examining Attitudes

Different REBT therapists practise REBT in different ways and it is difficult to offer any guidelines for how to develop creativity in helping clients to examine attitudes. However, here are some suggestions:

1. Watch DVDs of different REBT therapists practising REBT and in particular study how they examined their clients' attitudes.
2. Read transcripts of REBT therapists doing REBT and again focus on how they examined clients' attitudes (see Dryden 2021b, Dryden and Ellis 2003).

3. Use the 'friend technique'. Ask your client how they would respond to a friend who shares their rigid/extreme attitude and what arguments they would use to respond to these attitudes as expressed by their friend.
4. Develop a fund of stories, parables and mottoes that teach sound REBT principles that you can draw on with different clients.
5. Use visual 'props' while examining attitudes. For example I have a wooden letter 'I' with multicoloured dots to teach the client that they (the 'I') are comprised of many aspects (represented by the dots) and that no aspects of them can fully define the whole of them.
6. Consider using a number of vivid examination methods. For example, throwing a glass of water over yourself to show the distinction between acting foolishly and being a fool. However, do not use such methods with clients who want a serious, formal relationship with their therapist.
7. Use humour, ensuring that you poke fun not at the client but at the client's attitudes (Ellis 1977).
8. Use self-disclosure, focusing on how you learned to examine your own rigid and extreme attitudes, in particular. Humour helps with therapist self-disclosure as well.
9. Focus your attention on what each of your clients finds persuasive in examining their attitudes and use these persuasive arguments with them as therapy unfolds.
10. Discuss how best to examine attitudes with your supervisor.

Key Idea

Develop a genuine enthusiasm for examining clients' attitudes.

Notes

1 The choice-based examination method can also be used with the three extreme and non-extreme attitudes discussed in REBT.
2 See Part 6 of this book, which outlines good practice in dealing with a range of clients' doubts, reservations and objections to REBT concepts and process.

Chapter 64

Examine a Rigid/Flexible Attitude and the Relevant Extreme/Non-Extreme Attitude

A disturbance-creating attitude in REBT terms consists of a rigid attitude (absolute musts or shoulds) and one or more extreme attitudes that are derived from the rigid attitude (an awfulising attitude, an attitude of unbearability and a devaluation attitude towards self/others/life). A healthy attitude in REBT consists of a flexible attitude and one or more non-extreme attitudes that are derived from the flexible attitude (a non-awfulising attitude, an attitude of bearability and an unconditional acceptance attitude towards self/others/life). Only examining either the rigid/flexible attitude premise or the extreme/non-extreme derivative attitude means that the unexamined pair remains intact. Examining rigid and flexible attitudes does not mean that the derived extreme and non-extreme attitudes will be examined and vice versa.

After you have examined rigid/flexible and extreme/non-extreme attitudes, your clients may tell you that examining one rather than the other is more effective for them. If this is the case, encourage them to go forward examining the attitude pair that leads to greater therapeutic progress. However, still encourage them to examine the other pair some of the time.

Key Idea

Encourage your clients to examine both their rigid/flexible and extreme/non-extreme attitudes. However, some clients will find that examining their rigid/flexible attitudes is more meaningful for them than examining the extreme/non-extreme attitudes and vice versa.

DOI: 10.4324/9781003423348-69

Chapter 65

Use Didactic and Socratic Examination of Attitudes Appropriately

In Chapter 23, I discussed the use of Socratic and didactic methods when outlining REBT concepts to clients. The two most used styles use by therapists when helping clients to examine their attitudes are again Socratic and didactic.

In the Socratic style, you ask your clients questions regarding the logical, empirical and pragmatic status of both their rigid/extreme attitudes and their corresponding flexible/non-extreme attitudes (see Chapter 63).[1] Using the Socratic style, clients are helped to reflect on their attitudes; through this process, clients come to the eventual realisation that their rigid/extreme attitudes are false, illogical and are self-defeating, while their flexible/non-extreme attitudes are true, logical and self-enhancing.

The didactic style of helping clients to examine their attitudes (technically speaking, it is teaching you are undertaking) involves you presenting brief explanations to your clients as to why rigid/extreme attitudes are false, illogical and are self-defeating, while their flexible/non-extreme attitudes are true, logical and self-enhancing. When using this style, it is important to guard against talking a lot. Keep your explanations short and after you have finished teaching a substantive point, ask the client to put this point into their own words to assess their understanding of it. Then ask them what they think of the point. Remember that a client can understand an REBT concept, but not agree with it.

REBT therapists usually employ both. It is important that you assess which attitude-examining style is more productive with each client rather than move between the two styles when the mood takes you. In deciding upon a predominantly Socratic or didactic style of examining attitudes, assess your client's intellectual abilities (e.g.

DOI: 10.4324/9781003423348-70

unreflective clients might do better with a more didactic style while psychologically minded clients might profit more with a mainly Socratic style). Generally speaking, you can start with Socratic disputing supplemented by short didactic explanations until incoming information tells you to retain or alter this strategy.

> **Key Idea**
>
> Assess your clients' responses to the Socratic and didactic styles of examining attitudes to determine which style is the more productive for them.

Note

1 In Chapter 41, I argued that when assessing the presence of rigid and extreme attitudes, it is useful at the same to help the client understand what the flexible and non-extreme alternatives to these attitudes are. In Chapter 63, I outlined the choice-based examination method where the therapist helps the client examine side-by-side their rigid and flexible attitudes and their extreme and non-extreme attitudes. I present this simultaneous approach to examining clients' attitudes in this book while noting that other REBT therapists help clients examine their rigid and extreme attitudes first and their flexible and non-extreme attitudes later.

Chapter 66

Focus on the Type of Argument that Is More Helpful to Your Clients than the Other Types

Initially, you can encourage your clients to examine their attitudes using logical, empirical and pragmatic arguments (see Chapter 63). Clients do not usually find all three types of arguments equally helpful or insightful. When it becomes apparent to you which type(s) of argument your client responds to, phase out the type(s) that are less productive.

In the following excerpt, the therapist reviews the three types of arguments with the client:

Therapist: What did you think of the logical approach that it is not logical to rate yourself on the basis of your actions?

Client: Not much. It went over my head.

Therapist: And the realistic arguments about if you were really a failure, then all you could ever do would be to fail?

Client: I could see what you were driving at but still too much up in the air, if you know what I mean?

Therapist: I do. The pragmatic arguments were about how your life is likely to be, if you hold on to the attitude that you are a failure if you fail. I thought those arguments were helpful for you. Am I correct?

Client: You are. When you were asking me those sorts of questions, something clicked. I could imagine myself moping around all miserable for the rest of my life. I don't want that.

DOI: 10.4324/9781003423348-71

Therapist: Shall we stick with those kinds of questions?
Client: Yes, because that really brings it home to me.

Often, pragmatic arguments are the most persuasive because they itemise for clients the concrete consequences of continuing to adhere to rigid/extreme attitudes while point out that life would be much better for them if they develop an alternative set of flexible/non-extreme attitudes. However, it is important that clients themselves determine the persuasiveness of such arguments and can be encouraged to use these going forward.

Key Idea

Discover which type of attitude examination strategy your clients find the most influential in leaving behind their rigid/extreme attitudes and moving forward with the alternative set of flexible/non-extreme attitudes.

Chapter 67

Help Your Clients to Put Flexible/Non-Extreme Attitudes into Their Own Words

When your clients have committed themselves to going forwards with their new flexible/non-extreme attitudes, make sure it is in their language rather than in the lengthy and somewhat unwieldy statements found in some REBT textbooks, e.g. 'I would prefer to have your approval, but there is no reason why I must have your approval, and, if I don't receive your approval, this does not mean that I am inadequate but a fallible human being who can accept himself despite not being accepted by others'. Your clients' flexible/non-extreme attitude might be 'I'm fallible, too bad', which, when analysed, is based on a fully stated flexible attitude and an unconditional self-acceptance attitude (see Table 1 in the Introduction). The meaning behind the words is more important than the words themselves, so do not 'force' your clients into uttering unnatural pronouncements just because they accurately articulate REBT theory.

Having made this point, do ensure that your clients' individually stated flexible/non-extreme attitudes do reflect the meaning behind the 'lengthy and somewhat unwieldy' formally stated flexible/non-extreme attitudes.

Key Idea

Help your clients to put their flexible/non-extreme attitudes into their words, not yours or REBT's.

DOI: 10.4324/9781003423348-72

Chapter 68

Help Your Clients to Examine Attitudes Rather than Argue about Them

When you examine attitudes you encourage your clients to make a careful examination of their attitudes, both flexible/non-extreme and rigid/extreme irrational, in order to determine their self-helping or self-defeating nature. REBT therapists do argue with clients, in the sense of advancing arguments for their consideration, but not in the sense of quarrelling, picking a fight or wearing clients down until they 'give the right answer'. When you encourage your clients to examine their attitudes this does involve verbal persuasion on your part, but not verbal coercion.

REBT offers your clients new ways of understanding and tackling their problems. This usually involves a healthy debate about the pros and cons of change. If you believe you have to convince your clients of the correctness of your viewpoint, debate disappears and is replaced by arguing and power struggles. Clients are more likely to be convinced by the quality of your arguments and less likely through arguing (see the chapter entitled 'The Best Rational Arguments' in Hauck 1980). Therefore, in order to help your clients examine their attitudes without getting into an argument with you, keep your ego out of the discussion and focus on presenting arguments that your clients may find acceptable rather than persuading your clients in the correctness of REBT theory.

Key Idea

When examining your clients' attitudes, engage them in debate and avoid arguing with them.

DOI: 10.4324/9781003423348-73

Chapter 69

Take Care to Examine Attitudes Rather than Inferences

When you make inferences, you draw conclusions from your observations (e.g. your partner comes home late from work several nights in a row, and you infer she is having an affair, which you are upset about). Inferences can be seen as partially evaluative in nature because they imply an appraisal of a situation (a negative one in the above example). However, REBT views attitudes as the main cognitive determinants of our emotional responses, because they are fully evaluative in nature (e.g. 'My partner must not be having an affair. If she is, that would be awful'); attitudes are evaluations of our inferences. It is crucial to make this distinction between inferences and attitudes otherwise you may find yourself encouraging your client to examine inferences thinking they are attitudes, thereby leaving intact their clients' disturbance-inducing thinking.

Keep the distinction between inferences and attitudes clearly in your mind until it becomes second nature to you. What will also help you to examine attitudes rather than inferences is if you encourage your clients to accept temporarily that their inferences are true.

Client: My partner came home late from work several nights in a row. I think she is having an affair and I am very hurt about this.

Therapist: Let's assume temporarily that she is having an affair, let's examine your attitude, 'My partner must not be having an affair. If she is, that would be awful'

DOI: 10.4324/9781003423348-74

Compare this with the following interchange.

Client:	My partner came home late from work several nights in a row. I think she is having an affair and I am very hurt about this.
Therapist:	Other than coming home late, do you have any other evidence that she is having an affair.

Key Idea

Learn to distinguish inferences from attitudes and examine the latter, not the former.

Part 5

Good Practice in Negotiating and Reviewing Homework Tasks in REBT

Chapter 70

Negotiate and Review Homework Tasks

Homework tasks are an indispensable part of REBT. They allow your clients to put into daily practice the learning that occurs in therapy sessions, give them the opportunity to become more competent and confident in facing their problems, facilitate and accelerate their progress towards becoming their own therapist and enable them to act in ways that support their flexible/non-extreme attitude and undermine their rigid/extreme attitude. Burns (1989: 545) suggests that 'compliance with self-help tasks may be the most important predictor of therapeutic success'. Homework usually forms the bookends of the therapeutic agenda of second and subsequent sessions: reviewing the homework task is the first item on the agenda, while negotiating a homework task is the last.

Negotiating Homework Tasks

The following points are important to consider when negotiating homework tasks with your clients.

1. A rationale for the incorporation of homework tasks should be given to clients and discussed with them. It is still possible to do REBT with clients who do not want such tasks to feature in therapy. However, they should appreciate that therapy will take much longer without the regular execution of homework tasks than with them being done routinely.
2. Homework tasks should be negotiated with clients rather than assigned to them unilaterally. When clients have had an active role in the determination of a homework task, then they are more likely to do it than when it has been unilaterally assigned to them.

DOI: 10.4324/9781003423348-76

3. The negotiation of a homework task should flow logically from the work you have done with your clients in the session. Your clients are more likely to carry out their homework task when they see this link and how doing the task will take them a step forward towards reaching their goals.
4. It is also important that you devote sufficient time to their negotiation.

When you do negotiate homework tasks, ensure that you review them at the next session, otherwise you will be conveying to your clients that these tasks are actually unimportant or that you are uninterested in their progress. Therefore, do not be surprised if your clients fail to carry them out.

Reviewing homework involves extracting the learning from whatever has occurred – a 'win-win' formula.

1. Did the client carry out the homework task successfully? How was the client able to achieve this?
2. Did the client encounter any obstacles, and, if they did, how did they manage to overcome them?
3. The client did a homework task but not the agreed one. Why did the client change the task?
4. The homework task was quickly abandoned. What went wrong?
5. The agreed task was not carried out. What prevented the client from carrying it out?
6. Reviewing homework tasks teaches your clients how to do it as part of their developing role as a self-therapist.

Key Idea

Ensure that you negotiate and review homework tasks in every session.

Chapter 71

Make the Homework Task Therapeutically Potent

If your clients want to ingrain their new flexible/non-extreme attitudes and attenuate their old rigid/extreme attitudes, it is important for them to enter and stay in situations that they disturb themselves about. By using their flexible and extreme attitudes in these situations, clients can learn to undisturb themselves and thereby re-evaluate the 'horror' with which they previously viewed these situations. Moving too slowly through a hierarchy of feared situations can reinforce your clients' fears (e.g. 'I have to go this slow because I can't bear the discomfort involved in moving any faster'), while entering the most feared situation straightaway can be too intense for your clients and they terminate therapy because they are not ready for 'flooding' (implosion). Almost 40 years ago, I suggested a middle way between gradualism and flooding called 'challenging, but not overwhelming', i.e. tasks that are sufficiently stimulating to promote therapeutic change but not so daunting that they will inhibit clients from carrying them out (Dryden 1985).

In the following excerpt, the trainee negotiates a homework task that 'stretches' the client:

Trainee: You said that clearing out the spare room is mind-numbingly boring, but you need to get it done.

Client: That's true, but I can't bear doing boring tasks.

[The trainee helps the client develop a non-extreme alternative to this attitude of unbearability: 'It's difficult for me to bear doing boring tasks, but I can bear it and I will do so if it's worth it to me'.]

DOI: 10.4324/9781003423348-77

Trainee: So, how much time are you prepared to spend a day clearing out the spare room once you have got into the mindset of this new attitude?
Client: About an hour?
Trainee: How long will it take you to do it at that rate?
Client: About two weeks?
Trainee: So, four hours a day gets the job done in half a week.
Client: Yeah, but that's too much for me.
Trainee: What would be a challenge for you and not too much for you that you are willing to commit to?
Client: Two hours a day.
Trainee: Let's agree on that.

If homework tasks are not potent, then your clients will not make the progress they hope for from therapy.

Key Idea

Negotiate with your clients challenging but not overwhelming homework tasks.

Chapter 72

Take Your Clients through the Specifics of Negotiating Homework Tasks

When your clients agree to carry out a suitable homework task, you might believe that homework negotiation is now over (after all, what else is there to say?). However, if carrying out the agreed task remains rather vague (e.g. 'I'll get round to it sometime next week'), it can mean that your clients will forget to do it, or will do it if nothing more interesting intervenes at the time as the task is not at the forefront of their mind. If you allow homework to be set in this hazy manner, do not be surprised if your clients tell you at the next session that they have not done it. In the following dialogue, the therapist concentrates her client's mind on specificity:

Therapist:	You've agreed to carry out rational-emotive imagery whereby you want to move from unhealthy anger to healthy anger annoyance when you think about your boss's rudeness. Is that right?
Client:	That's right. I want to be able to stop seething about it and start being assertive with him.
Therapist:	Now, we've practised the imagery in the session; when will you practise it in the following week?
Client:	Every day.
Therapist:	Where will you do it?
Client:	At home in the evenings and at work in my lunch break.
Therapist:	How often will you do it?
Client:	Twice at work and twice in the evening.
Therapist:	For how long on each occasion?
Client:	Ten minutes.

DOI: 10.4324/9781003423348-78

Therapist:	Any potential or actual obstacles to carrying out the imagery?

[This phase of homework setting is known as troubleshooting.]

Client:	I might forget because I am a busy person.
Therapist:	What will help you to remember?
Client:	I could write REI [rational-emotive imagery] in my diary for work and stick a note on my desk in the study at home.
Therapist:	I presume you look in your diary and sit at or go to your study desk every day?
Client:	Without fail.
Therapist:	Any other obstacles?
Client:	None that I can think of.
Therapist:	But, if a new obstacle does occur…?
Client:	Do the problem-solving we've just done.
Therapist:	Why not make a note of the homework we have agreed in your therapy notebook?
Client:	Will do.

The specifics of homework negotiation include:

- The nature of the agreed task and its purpose
- When they will do the task
- How often the client will do the task
- The duration of each task episode
- Where the client will do the task
- Listing potential obstacles and what the client will do either to prevent the obstacles occurring or in response to them occurring.

Thus, specificity, not vagueness, should guide homework negotiation, which thereby makes it more likely that your clients will commit themselves to executing the task.

One final point: as the therapist in the above example did, ask the client to write down the homework task and make a copy of it yourself in your client's notes. Having them make a note of the homework keeps them actively involved in their therapy and as it will be in their handwriting, this will remind them of what they have agreed to do and avoids the potential disagreements at the next session that might arise from a purely verbal agreement.

Key Idea

Be specific in negotiating homework and troubleshoot obstacles to homework completion.

Chapter 73

Encourage Your Clients to Use Force and Energy in Executing Their Homework Tasks

Ellis (1979) wrote about the importance of using force and energy to uproot clients' disturbance-creating attitudes. Clients frequently cling to their rigid and extreme attitudes with great tenacity, and tepid methods lacking in force and energy are usually ineffective to uproot such disturbed thinking (e.g. gentle self-affirmations like 'I am a worthwhile human being'). For example, using force and energy in examining attitudes of unbearability and bearability can powerfully convince your clients that what was previously perceived as unbearable by them is actually bearable, while acting in a way that supports the new healthy attitude rational belief. As another example, a client who is tempted to start smoking again tells herself, 'I desperately want a cigarette *but I don't damn well need what I desperately want*', and refuses the offer of a cigarette. She stays in the presence of people smoking in order to teach herself that she does not have to disturb herself about seeing others enjoying a pleasure she has chosen to deprive herself of.

Using force and energy helps your clients to move from intellectual to emotional insight into their problems (see Chapter 57); in other words, your clients have conviction in their flexible/non-extreme attitudes because their effectiveness has been demonstrated in a particular or range of problem areas.

Trainee:	So, you are going to actively court discomfort by placing a cream cake in front of you and not eating it to prove that you can keep to your diet. Now, what will you say to yourself in order not to eat it?

DOI: 10.4324/9781003423348-79

Client (weakly):	I would prefer to have it, but I'm not going to have it. I hope that will stop me.
Trainee:	That sounds rather weak. Try something with more force.
Client:	That cream cake can stay there until it rots. I may want it, BUT I'M NOT EATING IT!

Key Idea

Teach your clients to use force and energy in carrying out their homework tasks.

Chapter 74

Use Multimodal Methods of Change

A multimodal examination of attitudes involves using cognitive (e.g. rehearsing rational-coping statements), imaginal (e.g. rational-emotive imagery), behavioural (e.g. staying in aversive situations) and emotive (e.g. shame-attacking exercises) methods to promote constructive change. Such multimodal attitude examination increases the likelihood of removing disturbance-inducing thinking and internalising a healthy outlook. Also, examining attitudes on several fronts can make therapy more interesting for clients rather than advancing on a single front.

Trainee:	You're reading the self-help books and rehearsing your rational-coping statements on self-acceptance. How are you getting on?
Client:	Well, I understand the concept of self-acceptance, but nothing seems to be happening.
Trainee:	What about taking some action?
Client:	Great suggestion. I'm fed up being treated by some of my friends as a taxi: 'Can you take me here, can you take me there?': The next time it happens, I want to say 'No'.
Trainee:	And the coping statement behind saying 'No'…?
Client:	'If you no longer like me because of it, too damn bad.' That gets the juices flowing. I want to start practising self-acceptance, not just keep reading about it.
Therapist:	Will it help you to rehearse saying no while practising that statement in imagery first?

DOI: 10.4324/9781003423348-80

Client: Yes it would.

[Here the trainee has suggested reading, behavioural, cognitive and imagery assignment and the client responds well to these multimodal suggestions.]

Key Idea

Use multimodal methods of change to help your clients to overcome their emotional problems.

Chapter 75

Check Whether Your Clients Have the Skills to Execute Homework Tasks

You might assume that, if your clients have agreed to the homework task, they have the skills to carry it out. However, your clients might have agreed to carry it out without thinking through what will be actually required of them, and you may have overlooked this important point too. Overlooking skills assessment can mean homework failure.

In the following dialogue, the therapist teases out the client's level of skill with regard to being assertive with her overbearing partner:

Therapist:	So, when your partner starts bossing you around, you are going to act assertively towards him. Is that right?
Client:	I am going to speak up for myself. I've stayed quiet for too long.
Therapist:	Imagine I'm him. How are you going to assert yourself?
Client:	Listen here, stop ordering me around. How dare you!
Therapist:	That sounds more like anger than assertion to me. Assertion means standing up for yourself without anger. Do you genuinely want to be assertive with him or angry with him?
Client:	Assertive, but I don't know how.
Therapist:	Shall I suggest some skills practice in the session before you try it out with him. How does that sound?
Client:	Yes, please.

DOI: 10.4324/9781003423348-81

Key Idea

Check that your clients have the skills to execute their homework tasks. If they do not possess these skills, you will need to teach them.

Chapter 76

Encourage Your Clients to Do Homework Tasks, Not to 'Try' to Do Them

Clients frequently say that they will try to carry out their homework. This seems at first glance a perfectly reasonable reply. What else would you expect them to say? However, while trying suggests that they will make an effort, it also denotes a lack of commitment on their part because they have not yet grasped the philosophical implications of what real change actually requires from them: forceful and persistent action, not half-hearted attempts at it. It is important that therapists respond when clients use the 'T-word'.

Therapist:	When you say 'I'll try to do the homework', what do you mean by that?
Client:	I'll do my best, I'll try. That's what I mean.
Therapist:	How long have you been trying to overcome this problem?
Client:	About ten years.
Therapist:	Where has this 'trying' attitude got you with overcoming your problem?
Client:	Not far to be honest.
Therapist:	So, if you continue to try, are you likely to make much progress or stay as you are with your anxiety problems?
Client:	Stay with my problems.
Therapist:	Now, when this session is over, will you leave the room or try to? Will you drive home or try to?
Client:	I will leave the room; I will drive home.
Therapist:	What's the point I'm making?

DOI: 10.4324/9781003423348-82

Client:	Doing gets it done, trying doesn't.
Therapist:	To really drive home this point, for homework, do you want to note down every day what you actually do and what you try to do, but don't?
Client:	I think that would be very useful to get this difference clear in my mind.
Therapist (smiles):	At the next session, we'll review whether you did the task or tried to do it.

In this context, I often quote Yoda, the Star Wars character who said, 'Do or do not. There is no try!'

Key Idea

Discuss with your clients the differences between a trying and a doing outlook in effecting constructive change.

Chapter 77

Take Time Negotiating Homework Tasks

I have emphasised the vital importance of homework tasks in Chapter 70 but many trainees rush homework negotiation because they leave it to the last minute or two of the session. This usually means that the homework task is dictated by the trainee or high-speed negotiation results in confusion for the client.

It is critical that you make provision for homework negotiation in the structure of the session (it is a key agenda item) – ten minutes should suffice or even longer for novice REBTers. If a homework task has emerged earlier in the session and been agreed upon, you will still need several minutes at the end of the session to remind your clients of what they have agreed to do. If you are on an REBT training course, I would suggest that you practise homework negotiation with your fellow trainees, incorporating all the points made in this part of the book, and time how long it takes. This exercise should help you to see that homework negotiation usually takes longer than you anticipate it will.

Key Idea

Give yourself plenty of time to negotiate homework assignments with your clients. If you rush homework negotiation, you decrease the chances that your clients will carry out the task or carry it out successfully.

DOI: 10.4324/9781003423348-83

Chapter 78

Remember to Review Homework Tasks

In Chapter 3, I discussed setting a therapeutic agenda with your clients. As my REBT colleague once said, the structure of a good REBT session[1] is like a pastrami sandwich. Thus:

- Review the homework session negotiated in the previous session
- Do the work agreed with the client
- Negotiate a new homework task suggested by the work done

Thus, ideally, you should begin every REBT session by reviewing the previously agreed homework task, and your clients should expect that this will happen. As previously mentioned, if you do not do this, you will convey a mixed message to your clients: homework tasks are important enough to negotiate but not important enough to review. Be aware that if you do not review these tasks, clients are less likely to do them than they would if you do review the tasks routinely. Having said that, do not make it mandatory that your clients do homework tasks. Remember that REBT is against almost all forms of dogma. Making homework mandatory is dogmatic. Stress that homework tasks are a vital part of REBT, but not mandatory.

How to Review Homework Tasks

There is no single way to review homework tasks with clients and different REBT therapists do this in different ways. It is more important that you review homework tasks than how you do so. Having made this point, here are several ways to review homework tasks:

DOI: 10.4324/9781003423348-84

- Say to your client, 'Let's begin the session by reviewing your homework task'
- Ask your client, 'What did you do for homework?'
- Read out to your client the agreed homework task and then ask what they did and how it went
- Particularly if your client made a written note of the homework task at the end of the last session, ask them what the task was and then ask them what they did and how it went.

When *Not* to Begin Therapy Sessions by *Reviewing* Homework Tasks

As mentioned above, REBT is against almost all forms of dogma. While it is vital for you to review homework tasks at the beginning of a session, it is not mandatory that you do so. What are the instances when you would *not* begin an REBT session by reviewing homework tasks with clients?

1. When the client comes into the session in a very distressed state. If you ignore their distress and begin by reviewing their homework task, you convey that you are indifferent to their distress, which will threaten your working alliance with that client. Attend to their distress and then, if appropriate, review the homework task.
2. When the client indicates that they have made a suicide attempt in the previous week or are currently suicidal. To ignore this and begin by reviewing the previous week's homework task would be inhumane and bad practice. Indeed, in some clinics, it is routine to begin every session with a mood check with all clients and then review homework tasks. You may not wish to begin a therapy session with a mood check with all of your clients, but you will want to do so with clients who you know are or have been suicidal.
3. A small minority of clients will not agree to do homework tasks. For these clients, doing homework tasks plays no part in therapy. While some therapists will refuse to see such clients, I do not recommend such a response. You can help such clients, but it will take longer to do so than it would if they carried out agreed homework tasks. It is important for such clients to accept the longer timescale. Given their stance on homework tasks and your agreement to go along with this stance, it would make no sense for you to begin

therapy sessions with reviewing homework tasks. Having said this, some of this small minority of clients are reactant, meaning that they are sensitive to perceived attempts to control them. They will do things to help themselves between sessions but will not view them as homework tasks. With such clients, I review what they have done between sessions, but do so informally and not at the beginning of therapy sessions. When I do so, I make no reference of the term 'homework tasks'.

Key Idea

Routinely begin each therapy session by reviewing clients' homework tasks unless you have a good reason not to do so.

Note

1 This refers to the second REBT session and beyond. As you have met the client for the first time in the first session there has been no homework task to review.

Chapter 79

Respond to Clients' Differing Experiences with Homework Tasks

When your client answers your query about what they did for homework, it is important that you listen carefully to their answer. In particular, you will want to discover:

1. Did they do the task or not?
2. If they did the task, did they do the task as agreed, or did they modify it in some way?

The 'No-Lose' Concept

It is worth bearing in mind the 'no-lose concept' when reviewing a client's homework task. First, if they did the task in its entirety, then this is good because they will make progress towards their goal. Second, if they completed some of the task but not all of it or they modified it in some way, then this is good because while they will make some progress towards their goal, their partial completion or modification tells you both more about the problem and their stance towards dealing with it. You can use this information to make any changes to your agreed treatment plan. Finally, if the client did not do the homework assignment at all, then while that is not good for them in the sense that their progress towards their goal will be minimal, it is good in the sense that it tells you both about their stance towards that homework task in particular and it may tell you something about their stance to homework tasks in general.

DOI: 10.4324/9781003423348-85

When the Client Did the Task and Did It as Agreed

When the client did the task and did it as negotiated, then they should be complimented on their achievement and you should focus your attention on what they learned from doing the task that they can carry forward. If the major item for the agenda is the same nominated problem, you have an opportunity to help the client take their learning from doing the homework assignment and apply it to the discussion that you are about to have on the same problem.

When the Client Did the Task but Did So Partially or Modified It

It often happens that the client did the agreed task but either did so partially or modified it in some way. The best way to respond to this situation is to compliment the client on doing some of the task, find out what they learned from doing what they did and then discover reasons why they did the task partially or modified it.

Therapist: OK so let's start with reviewing your homework task. What did you agree to do for homework?

Client: To start work on my essay at 2 pm on three days a week and work for three hours each day. I was to rehearse the attitude I don't have to be comfortable before I start work.

Therapist: How did it go?

Client: Pretty good I did it for the first two days, but not for the third.

Therapist: So a mixed experience. Well done for doing it for two days. Did you rehearse the attitude before starting?

[The therapist compliments the client for doing some of the task.]

Client: Yes, I did.

Therapist: What did you learn from doing the task?

Client: That I can start a tedious task even though I'm uncomfortable, and also that once I get it into the task, it becomes less tedious.

[The therapist asks the client for their learning from doing the homework task on the first two days.]

Therapist: Important learning. Let's look at what happened on Day 3.

Client: Well, I was pleased with the fact that I did the task for two days and on the third day, I remember thinking, 'I can't be bothered doing it today'. So, I didn't do it.

Therapist: Did you respond to that thought when you had it.

Client: No, I just went with it.

Therapist: If you had responded to it, what would you have said?

Client: 'OK so you can't be bothered. You can begin the task even though you can't be bothered'.

Therapist: What would have done if you had responded like that?

Client: I would have begun the task as I did the previous two days.

Therapist: So, what can you take away from that?

Client: When I think I can't be bothered doing something, that is not necessarily the end of the matter. I can respond to that thought and then do the task even though I can't be bothered doing it.

[The therapist Socratically helps the client to understand the reason why they did not do the task on the third day and helps the client see that they can respond to the obstacle to task completion and then act on that response to do the task.]

Therapist: And in the same way that you learned that when you begin the task uncomfortably that discomfort will go and you will get into the task, perhaps you will discover the same is true with the 'can't be bothered' thought. That you can begin the task even though you can't be bothered to do so and when you get into the task perhaps that can't be bothered thought and feeling will go.

[Ther therapist links the client's learning from partially doing the task and raises its relevance to what the client has learned from why they did not do the task on third day.]

Client: I'll try it and report back.

When the Client Did Not Do the Task

While homework has a vital role to play in the change process in REBT, it happens that clients will report that they did not do the task that they negotiated with you at the end of the previous session. It is very important that you investigate this with clients, but you do so in a way that encourages them to give authentic responses. If clients feel on the defensive in response to your enquiries, they will likely give excuses which will help neither of you.

Therapist: OK so let's start with reviewing your homework task. What did you agree to do for homework?
Client: Well, I agreed to approach my tutor to tell her that I am behind in my work while reminding myself that this did not prove I'm useless.
Therapist: OK. How did it go?
Client: I didn't do it.
Therapist: OK, can you help me understand why not?
Client: I'm not sure myself.
Therapist: Shall we figure out why together?
Client: That would be good.

[The therapist's response to the client is initially matter-of-fact and then invites the client to work with them to discover reasons for the non-completion of the task. The working alliance between them is thus preserved.]

Therapist: When we were negotiating the task last week, how did you feel about what we were doing?

[The therapist decides to develop a timeline to understand at what point the client decided not to do the task.]

Client: I felt good about what we were doing and I felt you involved me in the task negotiation.

Therapist: So, you are OK with the role of homework tasks in therapy in general?

Client: Yes, that makes sense and was one of the reasons I was looking for a more focused approach to therapy.

Therapist: And you were OK with the specific task that we agreed on?

Client: Yes, I was fine with it.

Therapist: Did you have a specific time in mind to approach your tutor?

Client: No…and I think it would have been better if I had…I just let it ride.

Therapist: If we discussed a time for you to do the task would that have made any difference?

Client: Actually, yes.

Therapist: So, if we had agreed a time when you would have seen your tutor, you would have done the task?

Client: Yes.

Therapist: So, what can we both learn from that?

Client: To be specific not only about what I am going to do for homework but when I am going to do it.

Therapist: That is good learning for me too.

[Through patient questioning the therapist helps the client to discover the reason for non-completion of their agreed homework task. Note how the therapist shares responsibility for not agreeing a specific time for the task to be done, a point they can both use in their future work together.]

Key Idea

It is important to respond therapeutically whether the client has done the homework task i) in full, ii) in part or in modified form or iii) not at all.

Chapter 80

Capitalise on Successful Homework Completion

As discussed in the previous chapter, the obvious procedure to follow when your clients fail to execute homework tasks successfully is to discover what happened. It is also important to *capitalise* on successful homework completion.

Therapist: Did you get into the lift and go up two floors?

Client: I did, and it wasn't as bad as I thought. Actually, I could have gone all the way to the top, but that wasn't the agreed homework. It would have been great to do it, though.

Therapist: When we first discussed the strategy for overcoming your fear of lifts, we agreed that it would be slow and gradual. It sounds like you want to change that now. Correct?

Client: Yes, I do. I want to go all the way to the top floor in one go. I want that to be the next homework task.

Therapist: Agreed. Now, if you couldn't get to the top in one go…?

Client: I wouldn't be upset or despairing. I just know that I can do more to overcome this problem than I'm currently doing, and I want to get on with it.

Therapist: That's fine.

DOI: 10.4324/9781003423348-86

Key Idea

Capitalise on your clients' successful homework completion and their desire to quicken the pace of change.

Part 6

Good Practice in Dealing with Clients' Doubts, Reservations and Objections to REBT

Chapter 81

Elicit and Respond to Your Clients' Doubts, Reservations and Objections (DROs) to REBT

It is probable that many of your clients will have DROs to REBT. If these DROs remain unaddressed, these clients are likely to be influenced by them to the detriment of their own therapeutic progress in developing and/or internalising a flexible and non-extreme outlook. These DROs can involve any aspect of REBT. Just because clients understand REBT concepts it does not follow that they agree with them and therefore it is good practice for therapists to elicit and respond to their clients' REBT-based DROs.

Client: So, discomfort tolerance is about learning to endure, putting up with things without having to like them.

Therapist: That's right. Do you have any objections to learning discomfort tolerance?

Client: Actually, I do. If I'm just supposed to put up with everything, then my life will be an endless struggle: just grin and bear it. I'm not excited by that prospect at all. I might as well give up therapy now.

Therapist: Thank you for that feedback. Discomfort tolerance is not meant to be a life of grim endurance but learning to bear those things that you currently believe are unbearable in order to reach your goals. So, learning discomfort tolerance is directly related to helping you to achieve your goals.

[The therapist responds to the client's objections non-defensively and corrects their misconceptions about discomfort tolerance.]

DOI: 10.4324/9781003423348-88

Client:	So, discomfort tolerance would help me to get on with this immensely boring paperwork thereby meeting my deadlines – which is my goal – instead of missing them. Is that right?
Therapist:	Correct. Do you want to see how to put discomfort tolerance into practice?
Client:	Now that we've cleared things up, yes, I do.

Key Idea

Remember that your clients will have doubts, reservations and objections to REBT, so elicit and respond to them in a non-defensive manner. Unaddressed doubts, reservations and objections are likely to hinder or derail your clients' progress.

Chapter 82

Deal with Your Clients' Doubts, Reservations and Objections (DROs) to Giving Up Rigid Attitudes and Acquiring Flexible Attitudes

Clients can and often do harbour DROs to:

- Surrendering their rigid attitudes and each of the three extreme attitudes derived from these rigid attitudes.
- Acquiring flexible attitudes to these rigid attitudes and each of the non-extreme attitudes derived from these flexible attitudes (Dryden 2022b).

Here I focus on clients' DROs to doubts surrendering their rigid attitudes and acquiring flexible attitude beliefs and in Chapters 83–85, I will deal with similar DROs concerning each of the extreme/non-extreme attitude alternatives.

In my experience, clients tend to harbour one major doubt, reservation and objection to surrendering their rigid attitudes and acquiring their flexible alternative attitudes:

> A rigid attitude helps motivate me to achieve what I want, while the flexible alternative attitude doesn't. Therefore, if I give up my rigid attitude in favour of my flexible attitude, I'll lose the motivation to do what is important to me.

For other doubts, etc., see Dryden (2022b).

In the following excerpt, a more experienced REBT therapist deals with this doubt Socratically and, as it transpires, effectively.

Therapist: So, what do you think about working towards believing 'I want to pass my exam, but I don't

DOI: 10.4324/9781003423348-89

have to do so' as a healthy alternative to your attitude 'I must pass my exam'?

Client: I'm not sure.

Therapist: What's your doubt?

Client: That this new belief won't motivate me to revise for my exam.

Therapist: If this were true, then I can understand why you would be reluctant to give up your rigid attitude and to acquire your flexible attitude. However, luckily this is not the case. Can I explain?

Client: OK

Therapist: Well, your rigid attitude has two components, one which spells out your desire (i.e. 'I want to pass my exam…') and the other one which makes your desire rigid ('…and therefore I must pass it'). Can you see that?

Client: OK.

Therapist: Does the desire part give you the motivation to study?

Client: Yes, it does.

Therapist: What about the rigid part?

Client: Well, it does, but in a very unproductive way.

Therapist: In what way?

Client: It makes me anxious.

Therapist: So, which part do we need to keep and which do we need to change?

Client: So, we need to keep the desire part, but find an alternative to the rigid part.

Therapist: OK. Let's look at the two components of the flexible attitude alternative. It has the same desire part as your rigid attitude (i.e. 'I want to pass my exam…') but the second part which prevents the attitude from becoming rigid (i.e. '…but I don't have to pass it'). Can you see that?

Client: Yes.

Therapist: Now we know that the rigid component (i.e. '… and therefore I must pass my exam') leads to

	anxiety. What effect does the non-rigid component (i.e. '…but I don't have to pass it') have on you?
Client:	Well, I won't be anxious, but it will stop me being motivated. Won't it?
Therapist:	Well, the desire part will keep you being motivated. The non-rigid part will take away the anxiety, not your motivation.
Client:	Oh yes, I didn't see that.
Therapist:	So, with your rigid attitude you will be motivated, but with anxiety and with your flexible attitude, you will also be motivated, but without anxiety. That's your choice. Which do you want?
Client:	Motivation without anxiety.
Therapist:	So that's a vote for your flexible attitude?
Client:	Yes, it is.

The therapist in the above exchange has done the following:

1. They take the client's original doubt seriously.
2. They take the client's rigid attitude and shows the client that it has two components: a desire component and a rigid component and helps them to see that the problem with motivation is with the rigid component (i.e. it leads to anxiety).
3. The therapist then shows the client that their flexible alternative belief has the same productive desire component and a different non-rigid component. The therapist helps the client to see that while they will still be motivated with this attitude (the desire component will take care of that), they will not be anxious (the non-rigid component prevents anxiety).
4. You will note that the therapist does not introduce the issue of concern resulting from the flexible attitude. They do not do so, because it would interfere with the teaching point: the client's flexible attitude does not stop them being motivated to revise for their exam.

When your clients have doubts, reservations and objections to surrendering their rigid attitudes and acquiring flexible attitudes, they may not readily disclose such doubts, etc., but will often display their doubts indirectly. You can make mistakes if you fail to spot these signs or if you spot them, you may think erroneously that because your clients have not expressed a doubt directly, you don't have to deal with it.

Key Idea

When your clients have doubts, reservations or objections to surrendering their rigid attitudes and acquiring and developing flexible alternatives to these attitudes, help them to understand clearly the components of both attitudes and use these components to dispel their doubts.

Chapter 83

Deal with Your Clients' Doubts, Reservations and Objections (DROs) to Giving Up Awfulising Attitudes and Acquiring Non-Awfulising Attitudes

Dealing with your clients' DROs to surrendering an awfulising attitude and acquiring an alternative non-awfulising attitude instead will help prevent your clients from grossly exaggerating the negativity of an adversity and the dire consequences of doing so. The following is the most commonly expressed client doubt in this area:

> My awfulizing attitude shows that what has happened to me is tragic while the non-awfulizing attitude makes light of this tragedy. Therefore, if I surrender my awfulizing attitude in favour of the non-awfulizing alternative, I am making light of what is tragic about my life.

In the following excerpt, the therapist breaks down a non-awfulising attitude into its component parts to show the client that their doubts about surrendering their awfulising attitude in favour of its alternative non-awfulising attitude are misconceived.

Therapist:	What's your reaction to working towards adopting the attitude, 'It's very bad to be diagnosed with diabetes, but not awful', rather than the idea that 'It's awful to be diagnosed with diabetes'?
Client:	I'm not keen.
Therapist:	Why?
Client:	Because it minimises the tragedy for me of getting diabetes.

DOI: 10.4324/9781003423348-90

Therapist: OK. Can I make an important distinction between the terms 'tragic' and 'awful' as they are used in REBT?

Client: OK.

Therapist: 'Tragic' refers to something that has happened in your life that is highly aversive and which has changed your life for the worse, but has not irrevocably ruined it. Although the event is 'tragic', you can transcend it and go on to live a life with some meaning and happiness. 'Awful', on the other hand, means that something has happened to you that has irrevocably ruined your life which you cannot transcend. As a result, your life is devoid of meaning and the possibility of happiness. Does that make sense to you?

Client: Yes.

Therapist: So, holding a non-awfulising attitude enables you to acknowledge that being diagnosed with diabetes is tragic, but not awful according to the distinction that I have just made.

Client: So, from what you say it seems that the non-awfulising attitude helps me to come to terms with the tragedy of my diagnosis and to get on rebuilding my life, whereas holding an awfulising attitude means that I think that my life is over and there is nothing that I can to do rebuild it.

Therapist: Exactly.

Client: Then, can you help me to acquire the non-awfulising attitude please?

Therapist: Sure.

By carefully articulating the components of a non-awfulising attitude, the therapist helps the client to see that such an attitude does not make light of tragedy. Indeed, it helps the client to acknowledge that a tragedy has happened to them, but gives them hope that they can rebuild their life. On the other hand, the client is helped to see that their awfulising attitude turns a tragedy into an end of the world experience which they can never get over. Consequently, the client decided to surrender their awfulising attitude in favour of the non-awfulising attitude alternative, since they could clearly see that in doing so, they would not be making light of what they saw as tragic.

Key Idea

When your clients have doubts about surrendering their awfulising attitudes and acquiring and developing non-awfulising alternatives to these attitudes, help them to understand clearly the components of both attitudes and use these components to dispel their doubts.

Chapter 84

Deal with Your Clients' Doubts, Reservations and Objections (DROs) to Giving Up Attitudes of Unbearability and Acquiring Attitudes of Bearability

Dealing with your clients' DROs to surrendering an attitude of unbearability and acquiring an alternative attitude of bearability instead will help prevent your clients avoiding dealing with adversities because they believe they can't bear to do so. The following is the most commonly expressed client doubt in this area:

> If I adopt the attitude of bearability I will learn to put up with aversive situations. My attitude of unbearability discourages me from putting up with these situations. Therefore, I am reluctant to give up my attitude of unbearability in favour of the alternative attitude of bearability.

In the following exchange, the therapist breaks down an attitude of bearability into its component parts to show the client that their doubts about surrendering an attitude of unbearability in favour of the alternative attitude of bearability are misconceived.

Therapist:	So, what are your views about working towards 'I can bear being passed over for promotion and it's worth it to do so' as opposed to your currently held attitude: 'I can't bear being passed over for promotion'?
Client:	I am not so sure I want to do that.
Therapist:	Because?

DOI: 10.4324/9781003423348-91

Client: Because it seems to me that the attitude of bearability will just help me to put up with it.

Therapist: I see. Can I make an important point about the meanings of 'bear'?

Client: OK.

Therapist: It is true that holding an attitude of bearability enables you to bear being passed over for promotion, but it is important that you understand clearly what 'bearing' means here. It does not mean putting up with being passed over for promotion without attempting to change it. Rather, it means putting up with it while thinking objectively, clearly and creatively about ways of effectively changing it. Is that clear?

Client: You mean that if I put up with being passed over for promotion, it will help me to deal with this aversive situation?

Therapist: Yes. Now, if it transpires that you cannot change this situation, your attitude of bearability will encourage you to put up with it without disturbing yourself about it. By contrast, your attitude of unbearability towards being passed over for promotion means that you find the situation unbearable. Will that lead you to deal with the situation objectively or will it lead you to take impulsive, unconsidered action to try to change the situation that will, in all probability, make the situation worse?

Client: Holding an attitude that I can't bear it will lead to me taking impulsive action. I normally do that and it rarely helps me.

Therapist: What happens if you hold this attitude and you can't change the situation?

Client: It drives me crazy. I can't settle and concentrate on anything.

Therapist: So, which attitude would you like me to help you go forward with?

Client: Definitely, the attitude of bearability.

By carefully spelling out what an attitude of bearability really entails, the therapist helps the client to see that they can put up with an aversive situation as a means of changing it if it can be changed or as a healthy way of adjusting to it if it can't be changed. By contrast, the client sees that their attitude of unbearability tends to decrease their chances of changing the aversive situation and increases the chances that they will disturb themself in some way if it continues to exist.

Key Idea

When your clients have doubts about surrendering their attitudes of unbearability and acquiring and developing alternative attitudes of bearability, help them to understand clearly the components of both attitudes and use these components to dispel their doubts.

Chapter 85

Deal with Your Clients' Doubts, Reservations and Objections (DROs) to Giving Up Devaluation Attitudes and Acquiring Unconditional Acceptance Attitudes

Dealing with your clients' DROs to surrendering a devaluation attitude and acquiring an alternative unconditional acceptance attitude instead helps prevent clients from devaluing themselves, others and life. The following is the most commonly expressed client DRO concerning a self-devaluation attitude (for example) and its healthy alternative unconditional self-acceptance attitude.

> Accepting myself unconditionally means that I don't need to change aspects of myself that I am not happy with or that I can't do so. Devaluing myself, on the other hand, motivates me to change. Therefore, adopting an unconditional self-acceptance attitude discourages personal change, while keeping my self-devaluation attitude encourages such change.

In the following excerpt, the supervisee brings this issue to supervision because they are unsure about how to deal with this DRO when their client expressed it in therapy.

Supervisor: From what you say it seems that your client is confusing the term 'acceptance' with the terms 'resignation' and 'complacency'. What does unconditional self-acceptance mean in REBT?

Supervisee: Accepting yourself means acknowledging that you are a complex, unique fallible human being with good aspects, bad aspects and neutral aspects.

DOI: 10.4324/9781003423348-92

Supervisor: It also means that you can and are advised to identify aspects of yourself that you are not happy with and to change them if you can. Indeed, adopting an unconditional self-acceptance attitude will help you to change these aspects because it will enable you to devote all your energies to understand the factors involved and what you can do to change them. So, your client would say 'I tend to procrastinate and this proves that I am a fallible human being with good, bad and neutral aspects. Since procrastination is a negative aspect, let me see why I do it and what I can do to stop doing it'. What does resignation mean?

Supervisee: Resignation means not trying to change negative aspects of yourself because you are sure that you cannot change them.

Supervisor: Correct. So here your client would believe 'I tend to procrastinate and there is nothing that I can do to change this'. This is very different from what is meant by unconditional self-acceptance. What does complacency mean?

Supervisee: It means having an 'I'm all right, Jack' philosophy which discourages self-change because there is no need to change anything about you.

Supervisor: Can you see how this is very different from unconditional self- acceptance?

Supervisee: I can.

Supervisor: Now, holding a self-devaluation attitude actually discourages self-change. It means treating yourself as if you were a simple being whose totality can be rated rather than as a complex, unique fallible human being who cannot legitimately be given a global rating. It means that when you identify a negative aspect of yourself that you wish to change you devalue yourself for having this aspect.

Supervisee: So here my client would hold, 'I tend to procrastinate and this proves that I am an incompetent fool'.

Supervisor: So, adopting a self-devaluation attitude will stop your client from changing their negative aspects because rather than devoting all their energies to working to change them, they focus on their negativity as a person.

Supervisee: I see. So, instead of focusing on reasons why they tend to procrastinate and figuring out a way of dealing with these factors, my client dwells on what an incompetent fool they are.

Supervisor: Yes, their unconditional self-acceptance attitude has the opposite effect to what they think it does. It motivates them to change aspects of themself that they dislike rather than thinking that they don't need to change them or that they can't change hem. Their self-devaluation attitude also has the opposite effect to what they think it does. Why?

Supervisee: Because it prevents them from changing negative aspects of themself rather than motivating them to change these aspects.

Supervisor: Do you think you can show the client this the next time you see them?

Supervisee: Yes I can, thanks.

When it comes to dealing with a client's other-devaluation attitude versus the unconditional other-acceptance alternative attitude, the following is the most commonly expressed client doubt:

> Adopting an other-acceptance attitude means that I am condoning that person's bad behaviour. Devaluing that person shows that I am not condoning their behaviour.

In the following excerpt, another trainee brings this issue to supervision because they are unsure how to deal with this doubt when their client expressed it in therapy. The client was unhealthily angry about their boss's unfair treatment of them and was resisting the idea of an unconditional other-acceptance attitude as an alternative to an other-devaluation attitude.

Supervisor: When your client accepts another person, they are taking the same stance towards that person as they would if they held an unconditional self- acceptance attitude. Which means what?

Supervisee: It means that my client acknowledges that the other person is a complex, unique fallible human being with good aspects, bad aspects and neutral aspects and that their unfair treatment of my client is bad.

Supervisor: So, acknowledging that the other is a fallible human being for acting badly includes recognising that their behaviour was bad and thus this behaviour is not being condoned. When your client devalues the other person, it is true that they are not condoning the other's bad behaviour, but it is also true that they are condemning the other. Let's apply these principles to your client.

Supervisee: When my client holds an other-devaluation attitude towards their boss, they do not condone the boss's unfair treatment, but they do regard the boss as a rotten person for treating them badly. However, when my client holds an unconditional acceptance attitude towards their boss, they not only accept the boss as fallible, but also do not condone the boss's behaviour, which they acknowledge is bad.

Supervisor: Very good. Do you think you can deal with your client's reservation about going forward with an unconditional other-acceptance attitude rather than an other-devaluation attitude?

Supervisee: Yes, I can.

Key Idea

When your clients have doubts about surrendering their devaluation attitudes and acquiring and developing unconditional acceptance alternatives to these attitudes, help your clients to understand clearly the components of both attitudes and use these components to dispel their doubts, reservations or objections.

Chapter 86

Explore and Deal with Your Clients' Doubts, Reservations and Objections (DROs) to Giving Up Their Unhealthy Negative Emotions and Experiencing Healthy Negative Emotions Instead

While REBT theory clearly distinguishes between healthy and unhealthy negative emotions about adversities, clients may have different ideas about these issues. Leaving aside the issue of nomenclature (e.g. we do not have clear terms for healthy negative emotions in the English language), clients may have idiosyncratic reasons for not wanting to surrender unhealthy negative emotions and/or to acquire healthy negative emotions (HNEs).

Thus, when it comes to unhealthy negative emotions, they may believe that they should experience these feelings given the adversities at *A*. In such cases, it is important not only to help these clients see that there is a healthy negative alternative to their unhealthy negative emotions, but also to spend time exploring with these clients, the advantages and disadvantages of both sets of negative emotions.

Clients often have doubts about acquiring and developing HNEs which may not appear healthy to them. Some clients may indeed have, from the REBT viewpoint, unhealthy negative emotions about these HNEs. This point can slip your attention if you only listen for the 'healthiness' of the healthy negative emotion.

When discussing the benefits or appropriateness of experiencing HNEs, it is important to pay attention to clues from them that they do not agree with your viewpoint. In the following excerpt, the therapist picks up the client's reservation about working to feel 'annoyed' (HNE) rather than unhealthy anger.

DOI: 10.4324/9781003423348-93

Therapist: When you say 'I suppose so', that usually means a person has reservations. Do you have reservations about the healthiness of annoyance with regard to not getting the promotion?
Client: I shouldn't have felt anything. I like to take set-backs in my stride.
Therapist: How would you feel if Stranraer lose a football match this weekend?
Client: Nothing.
Therapist: Why?
Client: Because I don't care…Oh, I get it. I do care about getting promotion so I should feel badly about it.
Therapist: Good insight. You will feel bad. Now the question is do you want to feel healthily bad – in this case annoyed – or unhealthily bad – in this unhealthy anger?
Client: I'll go for being annoyed.

Key Idea

Remember to explore your clients' idiosyncratic reactions to experiencing unhealthy and healthy negative emotions. Correct your clients' misconceptions when these are revealed.

Part 7

Good Practice in the Working-Through Phase of REBT

Chapter 87

Help Your Clients to Become Self-Therapists in the Working-Through Phase of REBT

Working-through is defined by Grieger and Boyd (1980: 122) as:

> Helping clients work through their problems – that is, systematically giving up their irrational ideas – is where most of the therapist's energy and time are directed and where longlasting change takes place. Successful working through leads to significant change, whereas unsuccessful working through leads to no gain or to superficial gain at best. It is as simple as that.

The ultimate aim of REBT is for clients to become their own therapists for both present and future emotional and practical problem solving. Encouraging your clients to become self-therapists is promoted by you in transferring to them increasing responsibility for analysing and tackling their problems within the REBT framework of change. This means them becoming more verbally active in the sessions and taking the lead in identifying, assessing and dealing with their problems and, correspondingly, you becoming less active-directive while still keeping your clients on track. For example, using prompts (e.g. short, focused questions) instead of explanations, 'nudging' your client through describing an emotional episode in *ABC* terms and having them take the lead in suggesting a relevant homework task. However, many trainees still 'take charge' of problem-solving in the working-through phase, thereby inhibiting clients from learning what self-therapy means:

Client: I got anxious again yesterday when my boss asked to see me.

DOI: 10.4324/9781003423348-95

Therapist: How do you make sense of this problem using the *ABC* framework?

Client: Well, '*C*' is obviously my anxiety. Being asked to see my boss is the situation in which I felt anxious.

Therapist: Do you remember how to identify what you are most disturbed or anxious about at *A*?

Client (thinking hard): Follow through in my mind what the situation means to me, so he wants to see me then…er…he will comment upon my work…

Therapist: In what way will he comment on it?

Client: Oh, unfavourably. Right, he will criticise my work. So that's my *A*.

Therapist: Good, and now your rigid and extreme attitude?

Client: And, if he does, this will mean…I'm incompetent.

Therapist: Is that the whole attitude?

Client: Er…let me see…the must is missing. Right, the whole attitude is 'He must not criticise my work because, if he does, this will mean I'm incompetent'. That wasn't too difficult, after all.

Therapist: The more you practise these skills both in and out of the sessions, the quicker you will become your own therapist or problem solver.

The therapist then asks the client what questions would help them to examine their rigid/extreme and corresponding flexible/non-extreme attitudes and what homework task they would design to rehearse their flexible/non-extreme attitude in the workplace. The therapist would provide prompts if the client had difficulty answering these questions. As your clients take over the reins of therapy, you can reconceptualise your role as a consultant, coach, mentor or adviser rather than as a therapist.

Key Idea

At the earliest opportunity in therapy, encourage your clients to start adopting the role of a self-therapist.

Chapter 88

Discuss with Your Clients that Change Is Non-Linear

Some clients might assume that, once they start thinking in a flexible and non-extreme way, emotional disturbance will disappear from their lives. Change will be a smooth, pleasant and uneventful process. If you do not elicit and counter such a view, then clients will be shocked when they learn that this is not the case.

To avoid or minimise such 'shocks', prepare your clients for the vicissitudes of the change process by explaining to them the non-linear model of change:

1. *Frequency* – are your unhealthy negative emotions and counterproductive behaviours experienced less frequently than before?
2. *Intensity* – when your unhealthy negative emotions and counter-productive behaviours are experienced, are they less intense than before?
3. *Duration* – do your unhealthy negative emotions and counterproductive behaviours last for shorter periods than before?

Encourage your clients to keep a log of their unhealthy negative emotions and counterproductive behaviours and the situations in which they occur so they can measure emotional and behavioural change using these three dimensions. This log will help to provide evidence of change when some clients complain that none has occurred. The non-linear model of change underscores Albert Ellis's observation that we can make ourselves less disturbed, but never undisturbable.

DOI: 10.4324/9781003423348-96

Key Idea

Discuss the non-linear model of change with your clients to prepare them for the 'rocky road ahead'.

Chapter 89

Explain to Your Clients Cognitive-Emotive Dissonance Reactions to the Change Process

Clients frequently complain of feeling 'unnatural', 'weird' or 'strange' as they work towards attenuating their often deeply held rigid/extreme attitudes and internalising a flexible/non-extreme outlook. This phenomenon is often referred to as 'cognitive-emotive dissonance', trying to believe a new flexible/non-extreme attitude belief while at the same believing the old rigid/extreme attitude – 'they [clients] see a better way, but cannot yet actualise it, so they conclude they cannot possibly overcome their disturbance' (Grieger and Boyd 1980: 161). At this point, some clients are likely to terminate therapy to feel 'natural' again (i.e. return to their self-defeating thinking). Given this, it is important to prepare clients for these dissonant reactions and explain how to cope with them.

Client: I'm beginning to feel very awkward and strange trying to accept myself, when I've spent so much of my life putting myself down.

Therapist: You're entering a stage in therapy where your old ways of thinking and feeling are in conflict with your new ways of thinking and feeling. This conflict leads to those awkward and strange feelings you're experiencing.

Client: How long will it last?

Therapist: Let's just say for the sake of argument a couple of months, but longer for more deeply ingrained rigid/extreme attitudes. It's important to tolerate these feelings until they pass, persist with examining your attitudes when you put yourself

DOI: 10.4324/9781003423348-97

down and keep on striving for unconditional self-acceptance. This current strange state of yours will eventually change into a more natural and comfortable state, if you keep on practising your flexible/non-extreme ideas.

Client: So, put up with the strange feelings and persist with examining my attitudes and taking appropriate action until I get through this uncomfortable stage.
That's the message, right?

Therapist: Correct. What's your reaction to that?

Client: Well, I'd like to bypass that stage, but if that discomfort is part of change then so be it. I will bear it.

Therapist: As I say, 'If it ain't strange, it ain't change'.

Client: I like that. I can use that.

Key Idea

Prepare your clients for experiencing cognitive-emotive dissonance reactions as they move through the change process, and help them cope with these reactions.

Chapter 90

Discuss with Your Clients Attitude Change vs. Non-Attitude Change

Attitude change in REBT refers to uprooting demands and their extreme derivatives from your thinking and developing flexible and non-extreme alternatives to them (Ellis 1994). Such attitude change can be situation-specific, cross-situational or influence every area of your life. Non-attitude change includes inference change, behavioural change and situational change without underlying attitude change. Whether your clients pursue attitude change or non-attitude change in part depends on you discussing these different outcomes with them.

Client: I'm feeling less anxious now; so I think it's time to leave therapy.

Therapist: It's good that you're feeling better. What do you attribute that to?

Client: Well, when I think someone dislikes me, I ask myself, 'Is that true' and realise that it isn't.

Therapist: What you have done is made what we call an inference change. You infer that someone dislikes you, stand back and ask yourself if it's true and conclude it's not. So, you feel better. Do you see?

Client: Yes.

Therapist: But an attitude change would involve you accepting yourself if you have clear evidence that someone did dislike you. Can you do that?

Client: Honestly? No, I can't not yet.

Therapist: If you were to change your attitude from 'I'm unlikeable, if others dislike me' to 'I can accept myself irrespective of how others see me', then

DOI: 10.4324/9781003423348-98

	what effect would this attitude change have on you?
Client:	I would be less prone to anxiety and panic in the face of disapproval. At the moment, I am feeling better, but that's all.
Therapist:	Right. You are feeling better, but are you getting better as the originator of REBT, Albert Ellis (1972), would say?
Client:	I guess not. So, you are saying that I need to stay in therapy and work to change my attitude.
Therapist:	I am. But it will involve quite a lot of work. Why not think it over and let me know what you decide next week.

Key Idea

Ensure that you discuss with your clients the differences between attitude change and non-attitude change and the pros and cons of each.

Chapter 91

Distinguish Between Your Clients' Pseudo-Flexibility and Non-Extremeness and a Genuinely Flexible and Non-Extreme Outlook

A minority of clients will develop a pseudo-flexible and non-extreme outlook which usually interferes with their ability to effect meaningful emotional and behavioural changes in their lives. Such clients often become avid consumers of REBT books and other materials and become extremely knowledgeable about REBT's theory and practice. They can quote extensively from the REBT literature and are able to give all the 'right' answers when it comes to them examining their attitudes. However, they fail to put their knowledge into practice between sessions (Dryden 2009).

To distinguish between genuine and pseudo flexibility and non-extremeness, look for discrepancies between what clients say is their attitude and what they actually do.

Therapist: Your goal was to ask women out, but what stopped you was a fear of rejection leading to self-rejection. Now you've become self-accepting, you say you don't need to ask women out. I don't understand.

Client: Now that I'm self-accepting, I no longer fear rejection; so I don't need to ask women out to prove to myself what I now believe.

Therapist: Surely the real test of attitude change is putting yourself in the line of fire – in your case, to face rejection?

Client: Why bother proving what's self-evident? I am self-accepting.

DOI: 10.4324/9781003423348-99

Therapist: Self-acceptance is a means to an end, not an end in itself. Presumably, you still want to have a relationship with a woman. Correct?

Client: Correct.

Therapist: Self-acceptance is meant to help you ask women out. Have you actually asked any women out?

Client (quietly): No.

Therapist: Because…?

Client: I'm still scared of being rejected.

Therapist: Shall we work towards genuine self-acceptance and asking women out? Self-acceptance with ignition?

Client: Let's do that. Being alone is no fun.

Key Idea

Be on the alert for discrepancies between your clients' professed flexible and non-extreme attitudes and what a genuinely flexible and non-extreme outlook entails.

Chapter 92

Help Your Clients to Generalise Their Learning to Other Problematic Situations in Their Lives

An important way of helping your clients to maintain their therapeutic gains is by encouraging them to generalise their REBT learning from problems they have tackled successfully to other areas in their lives. For example, if your clients have overcome their discomfort intolerance about meeting deadlines at work, they can then transfer what they have learned to other related situations in their lives, such as impatience in traffic jams or long queues.

Most of your clients will need help with this generalisation process. I discovered this many years ago when I was working with a young man who was anxious about being told off by his boss. We worked well together on this issue, and I helped him to develop a flexible and non-extreme attitude towards this adversity, which he implemented and was pleased with the outcome. Two weeks later, he came back to see me, and we had this interchange.

Windy: Nice to see you again. How can I help you today?

Client: Well, all was going well until a few days ago when I dropped and broke a plate while washing up and my wife told me off and I am really anxious that she might tell me off again.

Windy: That seems very similar to your anxiety problem about being told off by your boss, doesn't it?

Client: I guess it does.

Windy: Did you apply the flexible and non-extreme attitude that we developed together and which you

DOI: 10.4324/9781003423348-100

	rehearsed that helped you deal with your anxiety about being told off by your boss?
Client:	No, was I supposed to?

This taught me an important lesson. Most clients will need active help to generalise from one problem-related situation to another and also to other related situations. So, learn from my experience and build generalisation. Doing so will help clients to carry more of the responsibility for identifying and examining their attitudes and implementing their flexible/non-extreme attitudes in specific situations and then in a broader range of situations. Ultimately, your clients should remember that when they are emotionally disturbed, they will usually have sneaked a rigid/extreme attitude into their thinking which needs to be detected, examined and changed to a flexible/non-extreme attitude. As Albert Ellis used to tell his clients, 'Whenever you are emotionally disturbed, cherchez le should, cherchez le must. Look for the should, look for the must and vigorously dispute it until you have changed it'.

Key Idea

Encourage your clients to generalise their REBT learning by explicitly teaching them how to do it.

Chapter 93

Help Your Clients to Look for Core Rigid/Extreme Attitudes

Another way of helping your clients to move from dealing with specific problems to more wide-ranging problems is to help them to identify, examine and change core rigid/extreme attitudes which are central self-defeating rules of living and to develop and go forward with alternative core flexible and non-extreme attitudes. Core rigid/extreme attitudes can be difficult to detect as they remain dormant during periods of stability in our lives. They are usually activated and enter our awareness when we experience emotional disturbance about key adversities. Helping clients to examine a situation-specific rigid/extreme attitude and its flexible/non-extreme alternative belief encourages them to deal more effectively with that specific situation, while helping them to examine a core rigid/extreme attitude and its flexible/non-extreme alternative usually means a number of adverse situations are tackled simultaneously. Clients who are able to detect and deal with their core rigid/extreme attitudes and implement the alternative core set of flexible/non-extreme attitudes are better placed to extend their REBT learning across a wide number of situations. You might believe that, after you have helped your clients to detect and examine a few situation-specific rigid/extreme attitudes and develop alternative situation-specific flexible/non-extreme attitudes, your job is done. However, situation-specific attitudes can be seen as specific forms of a core attitude. From this perspective, you have only been chipping away at the core attitude instead of demolishing tackling it head on.

In the following excerpt, the therapist believes there is more work to be done, if the client is interested.

DOI: 10.4324/9781003423348-101

Therapist: We've looked at situations where you agonised over a career change, getting out of a dull relationship and changing to a new make of car. Can you see a theme running through these situations?

[Looking for a theme(s) that connects several situations is one method of identifying a core rigid/extreme attitude.]

Client (musing): A theme. Hmm. I think it's to do with certainty.

Therapist: My hunch is that you hold an attitude something like this: 'I must be certain that, if I change things in my life, they must work out well for me, and, if they don't, my life will be awful.' Does that ring any bells?

[The therapist presents her hypothesis for consideration by the client.]

Client: That sounds pretty accurate. That's why it takes me a long time to make my mind up about things.

Therapist: We've discussed three situations that this attitude is connected to. Are there any others that you are aware of?

Client: Quite a few I can think of and probably more I can't think of at this moment.

Therapist: Do you want to tackle this core belief that extends into other problem areas in your life?

Client: I think I would. I know this agonising of mine wastes so much time, so much effort, and with virtually nothing positive to show for it.

The position I have taken in this book is to identify alternative flexible/non-extreme attitudes every time you help your client to identify a rigid/extreme attitude. This applies to situation-specific and core attitudes. So, the therapist in the above example would help the client to develop the following core flexible/non-extreme attitude which they can begin to apply to the adversities listed above: 'I would like to be certain that things work out well for me, but there is no reason why they must work out well for me. If they don't, my life will be made more difficult but not awful'.

In my experience, it is unlikely that one core rigid/extreme attitude underlies all your clients' problems. Typically, it is likely that they hold at least two or three such attitudes involving both ego and discomfort disturbance.

Key Idea

Make sure that you help your clients to look for their core rigid/extreme attitudes and help them develop core flexible/non-extreme attitudes to counter them.

Chapter 94

Help Your Clients Understand How They Perpetuate Their Core Rigid/Extreme Attitudes

REBT mainly focuses on how clients maintain their emotional problems rather than on how they were acquired. Core rigid/extreme attitudes may have been present since childhood or adolescence and have maintained a powerful 'grip' ever since. As part of REBT's psychoeducational approach, help your clients to understand how they perpetuate their core rigid/extreme attitudes. This perpetuation process occurs in three main ways:

1. *Maintenance of core rigid/extreme attitudes*, i.e. thinking and acting in ways that maintain the core attitude (e.g. a client who thinks they are a fool behaves in foolish ways to make others laugh, thereby reinforcing their self-image).
2. *Avoidance of core rigid/extreme attitudes*, i.e. the cognitive, emotive and behavioural strategies clients use to avoid activating painful affect (e.g. a client turns to drink to blot out facing the failures in their life, but the act of avoidance just reminds them 'I am a failure').
3. *Compensation for core rigid/extreme attitudes*, i.e. engaging in actions that appear to contradict the core attitude (e.g. a client drives themself relentlessly to prove they are competent but this strategy backfires and they 'burn out', confirming in their mind that they are incompetent).

In the following dialogue, the therapist helps the client get some clarity concerning how they maintain their core rigid/extreme attitude.

DOI: 10.4324/9781003423348-102

Client: No matter what I do, I never seem to think it's good enough; then I think I'm no good. There's no job I won't take on. Others shrink back but not me. Why can't I get over this 'I'm no good' idea?

[It seems the client is striving to compensate for her core extreme attitude of 'I'm no good'.]

Therapist: How long have you had this core attitude of 'I'm no good'?

Client: Since my late teens, I think.

Therapist: What have you been trying to prove since then?

Client: That I am good enough rather than no good.

Therapist: But no matter what you do, what you achieve, you can never shake off that 'I'm no good' attitude. Is that right?

Client: That's right.

Therapist: What seems to be happening, then, is that you try to prove to yourself that you are good enough, but when these attempts fail, you go back to putting yourself down. So, your activities help to keep alive your negative self- image. Is that how it works?

Client: Yes, it is. I seem to be like the hamster on the wheel in its cage who's going nowhere. OK. It's beginning to make sense; so what do I do about it, then?

It is important not only to help your clients to understand their own particular ways of perpetuating their core rigid/extreme attitudes but also to assist them to develop robust cognitive, behavioural and emotive strategies to halt and then reverse the perpetuation process. With the above client, they can learn self-acceptance (e.g. 'I'm neither good nor bad, just a fallible human being who is no longer going to rate myself, only my behaviour'), reveal to others that they have given up the 'self-rating game' and select only work that is important to them. Finally, the client can learn to enjoy themself rather than prove themself.

Key Idea

Teach your clients how they perpetuate their core rigid/extreme attitudes. Then show them how to halt and reverse this perpetuation process.

Chapter 95

Teach Relapse Prevention

As therapy draws to an end, REBT focuses on teaching clients relapse-prevention strategies. Relapse prevention helps clients to identify those situations (e.g. negative emotional states, interpersonal strife) that they could disturb themselves about and thereby trigger the re-emergence of their emotional and behavioural difficulties. It is highly likely that lapses will occur and, if you have not helped your clients to anticipate and deal with these lapses, they could easily lead to a relapse followed by your clients returning to see you, believing that their therapeutic gains have been wiped out (or so demoralised by this 'collapse' that your clients do not contact you).

Some novice REBT therapists avoid discussing relapse prevention because they believe it ends therapy on a pessimistic note.

Supervisor: Why pessimistic instead of realistic?

Supervisee: Well, the client has been doing so well, I just think it will dampen their spirits if I mention the possibility of their panic attacks reappearing.

Supervisor: If you don't discuss relapse and they do come back, then what?

Supervisee: I suppose the client might be overwhelmed by them because I haven't discussed or prepared them for the possible return of the panic attacks.

Supervisor: So, do you want to help your client to prepare for the possibility of post- therapy setbacks or just

DOI: 10.4324/9781003423348-103

enjoy the feel-good factor of seemingly successful therapy?

Supervisee: OK. I agree. The responsible and self-helping strategy is teaching relapse prevention.

Relapse prevention in REBT will be based on the skills you have already taught your clients and should be an important part of your treatment plan as 'outcome is increasingly measured not only by treatment success but by relapse prevention' (Padesky and Greenberger 1995: 70).

Key Idea

Do not forget the importance of teaching relapse-prevention strategies to your clients.

Chapter 96

Encourage Self-Actualisation When Your Clients Indicate It as a Goal

Self-actualisation is defined as 'realising one's potential; the continuing process of actualising or putting into practice one's aspirations rather than ignoring, denying or suppressing them' (Feltham and Dryden 1993: 170). REBT teaches clients not only to overcome their emotional problems but also to pursue self-actualisation if they want a more fulfilling life (Ellis 1994). Once your clients have overcome their presenting difficulties by internalising a flexible/non-extreme outlook, you can then discuss some of the goals that would bring them greater happiness in life.

Client: You know, now that I'm not ranting and raving at work anymore, I really am fed up with office politics: all the backstabbing – in fact, working for other people. My dream is to be self-employed.

Therapist: Do you intend to follow your dream?

Client: I've already handed in my notice. I'd be interested in your opinion.

Therapist: I think, where it's possible, people should fulfil their dreams. I would urge you to remember to problem solve in a healthy manner when you encounter obstacles to becoming self-employed.

Client: I know it won't be easy, and I'll remember my REBT learning, but I'm determined to give it a go.

Therapist: That's great to hear. One further point: when you do become self- employed, that won't be the end of the dream, so to speak, but will present new challenges and experiences for you. So, it's important

DOI: 10.4324/9781003423348-104

to have an open mind about what leading a happier life can involve as opposed to having a fixed view about what it must involve.

Client: I realise I need to be open-minded about what lies ahead, but what lies ahead will, I'm sure, be much more interesting and fulfilling than what I'm leaving behind.

Therapist: Please think of keeping in contact if you want to discuss your progress to what we call your self-actualisation goals.

Client: Thank you. I will.

Key Idea

Some of your clients will want to think beyond their emotional goals and discuss their aspirations for a happier life. Be alert to and engage in this kind of discussion.

Chapter 97

Do Not Sacredise Endings

The REBT approach to the end of therapy is consistent with its views on most therapeutic matters. It is flexible. REBT therapists recognise that for some clients, the therapeutic relationship has become a very important part of their lives and as a result the ending of this relationship has to be handled delicately and sensitively and planned well in advance. For other clients, the therapeutic relationship is not so important and thus, a more matter-of-fact approach can be taken. In addition, in REBT, ending therapy is not seen as a once and for all event. It is recognised that clients may stop therapy for a while and pick up again later, sometimes much later.

The important point here is that the best way to end therapy is determined by your assessment of the unique aspects of the work you have done with a particular client. It is therefore a mistake to approach therapy's end in a uniform way.

Supervisor: You seem to be troubled by my suggestion that your client needs to stop seeing you fairly soon and rely on their own devices as their own therapist.

Supervisee: I am.

Supervisor: Why?

Supervisee: In my previous training, I learned that all therapy endings have to be carefully planned because ending therapy for clients is a loss that must be grieved.

Supervisor: Where is your evidence that this is so for the client we are discussing?

Supervisee: I guess there isn't any.

DOI: 10.4324/9781003423348-105

Supervisor: In fact, there is evidence that it's important for this client to be their own therapist as quickly as possible, hence my earlier suggestion.

REBT trainees who have previously been trained in other therapeutic traditions find it difficult to adopt REBT's flexible and pragmatic approach to ending therapy. If this applies to you, examine the practice-related rigid idea that ending therapy with all clients has to be done in the same careful and delicate way and its flexible alternative that such planning is needed in some cases, but certainly not all.

Key Idea

Don't sacredise the end of therapy. Rather, adopt a flexible approach as you assess the best way to end therapy for each of your clients.

Part 8

Good Practice in Self-Maintenance as an REBT Therapist

Chapter 98

Look After Yourself

You might spend so much time helping others that you neglect looking after your own physical and mental welfare. For example, you do not undertake regular exercise, become a workaholic, drink and eat excessively, your sense of humour disappears and your irritability quotient (IQ: Burns 1980) rises sharply. In this extract, the supervisor comments on the supervisee's irritable manner:

Supervisor: On your recordings, you are sharp and impatient with your clients as if they are irritating you because they don't get to the point.

Supervisee: Well, I've got so many clients to see and they're always rambling on, so many books to read, essays to write, supervisions to attend. It's always pressure. I never get a moment's peace.

Supervisor: What do you think will happen if you continue not to 'get a moment's peace'?

Supervisee: The dreaded burn-out. I feel it's already on its way.

Supervisor: What good will you be to yourself, clients, family, friends, partner and so on, if you burn out?

Supervisee: I'll just be one sad, miserable person.

Supervisor: Do you want to get some balance back into your life? Learn how to pace yourself for the long term instead of running yourself into the ground?

Supervisee: What do I have to do?

Supervisor: What if I were to refer you to an REBT therapist?

Supervisee: Well, I'm definitely not applying it to myself, so I suppose I do need some help. OK.

DOI: 10.4324/9781003423348-107

A not-so-obvious form of self-neglect is not accepting your temperamental tendencies and, instead, condemning yourself for them. For example, a friend of mine has discomfort intolerance towards anything mechanical when it breaks down. They demand it should be instantly fixed rather than have to work out the solution for themself (they see themself as 'useless' for not having the patience to work it out). They doubt whether they will ever see the day when this response is entirely gone from their life. As Dryden and Yankura (1995: 128) observe:

> We hold that you will take more care of yourself if you identify your temperamentally based patterns and accept yourself for them. You can certainly work to curb the excesses of these patterns, but if you accept the fact that you will not be able to change the 'pull' of your temperament, you will relax and even celebrate your temperament as being part of your uniqueness.

Also, with regard to your temperament, find a job profile that suits it rather than goes against its grain. For example, I enjoy pursuing the 'life of the mind' through writing, teaching and training in an academic-related setting, whereas working in a retail setting selling washing machines or television sets would be for me 'lifeless and mindless'.

Finally, strive to be authentic with yourself and others. By being authentic with yourself, I mean not trying to convince yourself that you are other than you are, accepting your faults and limitations without despair and seeking to address them in a constructive way. Being authentic with others means allowing them to see your real self rather than a simulated self – the latter 'self' is often employed if you hold that you need others' approval or you want to hide your true feelings from them. Authenticity with self and others rests on unconditional self-acceptance – a key REBT principle for the maintenance of mental health.

Key Idea

Be the guardian of your own physical and mental wellbeing in order to maximise your happiness and minimise your unhappiness. This will impact positively on your work as an REBT therapist as well as on other areas of your life.

Chapter 99

Do Not Disturb Yourself about Your Clients' Disturbances

While concern and compassion are important qualities to display to your clients as they relate their problems to you, being too concerned and desperate to 'heal the client's pain' can lead you to becoming just as disturbed as your clients. At this point, your clinical competence will probably start to decline as you become more and more absorbed in your anguish.

Supervisor: How will your suffering for her lessen her own suffering?

Supervisee: She's been through so much, more than any human being should have to bear. It's just so unfair, just one tragedy after another.

Supervisor: She's had a lot of harrowing experiences, but you didn't answer my question. How will your suffering reduce hers?

Supervisee: At least it shows I care, but, no, my suffering has made no impact on hers.

Supervisor: When you say 'at least it shows I care', it seems to me you are confusing caring, which is a compassionate response to a distressed individual, with caring too much, which involves you becoming disturbed about their distress.

Supervisee: I think you're right. I have crossed the line into caring too much.

Supervisor: That is easily done. But isn't your therapeutic task to help her to bear the unbearable rather than

DOI: 10.4324/9781003423348-108

showing her, through your behaviour, that her problems are unbearable?

Supervisee: I'm sure that's what I'm doing. It's important to stay focused on her problems, not mine.

Supervisor: One other thing. When she goes out and your next client comes in, where's your attention?

Supervisee: Still with her and not on the client sitting in front of me; so I'm not helping this client either.

Supervisor: If you lose your objectivity and allow yourself to be sucked into the client's problems, you don't help her and the next client and your skills go out the window. Is that your goal as a therapist?

Supervisee: Of course not. In my next session recording, I hope to show you that I've regained my clinical focus and composure.

As Paul Hauck (1980: 238–9; original author's italics) has wisely noted:

> Pitying clients or despairing over how life or others have treated them, is best handled if you accept the rational idea that one does *not have to be disturbed over other people's problems and disturbances*. Get hold of that idea securely, think it through in great depth, and accept it as a wonderfully sane piece of advice…Stop pitying people and you will bring yourself back on the right track.

Key Idea

Learn not to disturb yourself about your clients' disturbances, thereby staying clinically focused on their problems rather than being distracted or absorbed by your own.

Chapter 100

Do Not Sacredise REBT

Sacredising REBT refers to treating it as a form of religiosity. Ellis (1983: 1) describes religiosity as:

> a devout or rigid belief in some kind of secular religion (such as Libertarianism, Marxism, or Freudianism) – that is, a dogmatic, absolutistic conviction that some political, economic, social, philosophic view is sacrosanct, provides ultimate answers to virtually all important questions, and is to be piously subscribed to and followed by everyone who wishes to lead a good life.

To sacredise REBT is to stop practising it, i.e. REBT's open-minded approach to knowledge is transformed by you into a rigid conviction that REBT is the supreme and unquestioned source of all knowledge for understanding and tackling our problems in life – you become closed-minded, in other words. If you adopt this dogmatic standpoint, you are likely to experience the following blind spots:

1. You will not see or look for any weaknesses in REBT theory or practice.
2. You will not listen to or will summarily dismiss criticism of REBT.
3. Your evangelical zeal will probably 'scare off' some clients, while others are viewed by you as inadequate or lacking 'real' commitment to change because they do not 'work hard enough' to embrace REBT as wholeheartedly as you have done.
4. You make yourself emotionally disturbed more easily (e.g. angry) when other therapists or some clients attack REBT, or friends and family poke fun at you when you try to teach it to them.

DOI: 10.4324/9781003423348-109

5. You start losing your sense of humour as fervour replaces fun in your sessions (when the previous use of humour was therapeutically appropriate).

In the following excerpt, the supervisor points out their supervisee's rigid practice of REBT.

Supervisor: In your session recording, you've told the client on several occasions that she must think flexibly. Doesn't REBT want to remove rigid thinking, not encourage it?
Supervisee: She has to get better, though.
Supervisor: How will that happen if, through your teaching, she replaces one rigid attitude with another?
Supervisee: But she's got to see that flexible thinking will solve her emotional problems.
Supervisor: Why has she got to see it? Why can't you present the options to her and allow her to make up her own mind?
Supervisee: What's the point of teaching REBT if the client doesn't use it?
Supervisor: But that's her choice. Do you want to deprive her of freedom of choice, freedom of thought?
Supervisee: Of course not, but she should see that REBT will help her. She keeps on resisting.

[The unspoken part of the supervisee's last sentence is probably '…as she absolutely shouldn't do'. Given the supervisee's train of thought, 'she should see…': is highly likely to be absolute too. With regard to his warped practice of REBT, the supervisee holds dogmatic ideas.]

Supervisor: Look, the bottom line is this: you're practising REBT in a rigid way, which goes against the teaching of REBT. In other words, you've made yourself a non-REBTer. Do you want to practise REBT in its proper and flexible way or be dogmatic in its use?
Supervisee: I want to be flexible in its use.

Supervisor: OK, good. I'd like to suggest that you start by reviewing the recording of this session and make a note of the interventions you made which were rigid and what you could have said to demonstrate the flexible use of REBT. OK?

Supervisee: OK.

Key Idea

Do not adopt an uncritical adherence to REBT. Keep your REBT critical faculties sharp and sceptical.

Chapter 101

Practise What You Preach

While it is possible to practise REBT when you don't agree with its ideas or when you agree with them but don't use them in your own life, it is better if you practise what you preach as a therapist. If you do, it is my contention that you will be a more effective REBT therapist than if you don't. We frequently come across examples of trainees not practising what they preach (we would assume that all health professionals are guilty of this inconsistency on some occasions).

If you do not use REBT in your own life, some of the following problems are likely to occur:

- REBT has intellectual credibility for you but no emotional conviction.
- You are unlikely to understand the difficulties that your clients have in translating theory taught in your office into daily real-life experience.
- You are being inauthentic with your clients.
- Your REBT skills are never honed by 'front line' service, i.e. you are a theoretical REBTer, not an experiential one.

In the following excerpt, the supervisor wonders when the supervisee will start practising REBT in their own life.

Supervisor:	I made some criticisms of your session recording and you said, the exact words were, 'I'm useless'. What's wrong with your conclusion?
Supervisee:	I don't understand.

DOI: 10.4324/9781003423348-110

Supervisor: Imagine your client was a counselling trainee who said the same thing as you just did, what would you say to them?

Supervisee: Well, I'd encourage them to focus on learning from their errors but without condemning themself as a person for making them. Self-acceptance, in other words.

Supervisor: Exactly. When are you going to start practising REBT on yourself?

Supervisee (sheepishly): I don't know.

Supervisor: What prevents you from using it with yourself?

Supervisee: Well, they're clients, and I'm not.

Supervisor: So, they need REBT, but you don't. You're still fallible and prone to emotional disturbance just like your clients. If you don't use REBT with yourself, it will stay up here *(tapping forehead)* and never get into your gut *(patting stomach)*. You'll be a poor role model for REBT.

Supervisee: I didn't train in REBT to turn out as a poor role model; so I will start using REBT with myself.

Supervisor: Good. Remember, it's not just starting practising but continuing it over the long term.

Key Idea

Practise what you preach!

References

Bernard, M. E. (1986). *Staying Rational in an Irrational World: Albert Ellis and Rational-Emotive Therapy*. McCulloch.

Bordin, E. S. (1979). The generalizability of the psychoanalytic concept of the working alliance. *Psychotherapy: Theory, Research and Practice, 16*, 252–260.

Burns, D. D. (1980). *Feeling Good: The New Mood Therapy*. William Morrow.

Burns, D. D. (1989). *The Feeling Good Handbook*. William Morrow.

Cormier, W. H., & Cormier, L. S. (1985). *Interviewing Strategies for Helpers*. 2nd Edition. Brooks/Cole.

DiGiuseppe, R. (1991). Comprehensive cognitive disputing in RET. In M. E. Bernard (Ed.), *Using Rational-Emotive Therapy Effectively: A Practitioner's Guide* (pp. 173–195). Plenum.

Dryden, W. (1985). Challenging but not overwhelming: A compromise in negotiating homework tasks. *British Journal of Cognitive Psychotherapy, 3*(1), 77–80.

Dryden, W. (1987). *Current Issues in Rational-Emotive Therapy*. Croom Helm.

Dryden, W. (1997). *Therapists' Dilemmas*. Revised Edition. Sage.

Dryden, W. (1998). Understanding persons in the context of their problems: A rational emotive behaviour therapy perspective. In M. Bruch & F. W. Bond (Eds.), *Beyond Diagnosis: Case Formulation Approaches in CBT* (pp. 43–64). John Wiley.

Dryden, W. (1999). *How to Accept Yourself*. Sheldon Press.

Dryden, W. (2009). *Skills in Rational Emotive Behaviour Counselling and Psychotherapy*. Sage.

Dryden, W. (2013). *The ABCs of REBT: Perspectives on Conceptualization*. Springer.

Dryden, W. (2021a). *Rational Emotive Behaviour Therapy: Distinctive Features*. 3rd Edition. Routledge.

Dryden, W. (2021b). *Windy Dryden Live!* Rationality Publications.

Dryden, W. (2022a). *Understanding Emotional Problems and Their Healthy Alternatives: The REBT Perspective.* 2nd Edition. Routledge.

Dryden, W. (2022b). *Reason to Change: A Rational Emotive Behaviour Therapy (REBT) Workbook.* 2nd Edition. Routledge.

Dryden, W. (2022c). *Windy Dryden Collected!* Rationality Publications.

Dryden, W. (2024). *Fundamentals of Rational Emotive Behaviour Therapy: A Training Manual.* 3rd Edition. John Wiley.

Dryden, W., & Ellis, A. (2003). *Albert Ellis Live!* Sage.

Dryden, W., & Neenan, M. (2004). *The Rational Emotive Behavioural Approach to Therapeutic Change.* Sage.

Dryden, W., & Neenan, M. (2021). *Rational Emotive Behaviour Therapy: 100 Key Ideas and Techniques.* 3rd Edition. Routledge.

Dryden, W., & Yankura, J. (1995). *Developing Rational Emotive Behaviour Therapy.* Sage.

Dryden, W., Ferguson, J., & McTeague, S. (1989). Attitudes and inferences: A test of a rational-emotive hypothesis. 2: On the prospect of seeing a spider. *Psychological Reports, 64*, 115–123.

Ellis, A. (1959). Requisite conditions for basic personality change. *Journal of Consulting Psychology, 23*, 538–540.

Ellis, A. (1972). Helping people to get better rather than merely feel better. *Rational Living, 7*(2), 2–9.

Ellis, A. (1976). The biological basis of human irrationality. *Journal of Individual Psychology, 32*, 145–168.

Ellis, A. (1977). Fun as psychotherapy. *Rational Living, 12*(1), 2–6.

Ellis, A. (1979). The issue of force and energy in behavior change. *Journal of Contemporary Psychotherapy, 10*, 83–97.

Ellis, A. (1983). *The Case Against Religiosity.* Institute for Rational-Emotive Therapy.

Ellis, A. (1991). Using RET effectively: Reflections and interview. In M. E. Bernard (Ed.), *Using Rational-Emotive Therapy Effectively* (pp. 1–33). Plenum.

Ellis, A. (1994). *Reason and Emotion in Psychotherapy.* Revised and Updated Edition. Carol.

Ellis, A., & Bernard, M. E. (Eds.) (1985). *Clinical Applications of Rational-Emotive.* Plenum.

Feltham, C., & Dryden, W. (1993). *Dictionary of Counselling.* Whurr.

Fennell, M. J. V. (1989). Depression. In K. Hawton, P. M. Salkovskis, J. Kirk, & D. M. Clark (Eds.), *Cognitive Behaviour Therapy for Psychiatric Problems* (pp. 169–234). Oxford University Press.

Grieger, R., & Boyd, J. (1980). *Rational-Emotive Therapy: A Skills-Based Approach.* Van Nostrand Reinhold.

Hauck, P. (1980). *Brief Counseling with RET.* Westminster Press.

Moore, R. H. (1988). Inference as "A" in rational-emotive therapy. In W. Dryden & P. Trower (Eds.), *Developments in Rational-Emotive Therapy*. Open University Press.

Padesky, C. A., & Greenberger, D. (1995). *Clinician's Guide to Mind over Mood*. Guilford Press.

Persons, J. B. (2012). *A Case Formulation Approach to Cognitive Therapy*. Guilford Press.

Rogers, C. R. (1957). The necessary and sufficient conditions of therapeutic personality change. *Journal of Consulting Psychology*, *21*, 95–103.

Walen, S. R., DiGiuseppe, R., & Dryden, W. (1992). *A Practitioner's Guide to Rational-Emotive Therapy*. 2nd Edition. Oxford University Press.

Wessler, R. A., & Wessler, R. L. (1980). *The Principles and Practice of Rational-Emotive Therapy*. Jossey-Bass.

Wills, F. (2008). *Skills in Cognitive Behaviour Counselling and Psychotherapy*. Sage.

Young, J. (2024). *No Bullshit Therapy: How to Engage People Who Don't Want to Work with You*. Routledge.

Index

For Product Safety Concerns and Information please contact our EU representative GPSR@taylorandfrancis.com Taylor & Francis Verlag GmbH, Kaufingerstraße 24, 80331 München, Germany

Printed and bound by CPI Group (UK) Ltd, Croydon, CR0 4YY
08/06/2025
01897005-0005